# Get More
# **INSPIRATION**

# Get More
# INSPIRATION

## Unexpected ideas to help you achieve

**WARWICK MERRY**

**Get More Inspiration**

First published in 2015 by Get More Pty Ltd
38 Winmalee Drive, Glen Waverley, VIC 3150
GetMore.com.au

© Warwick Merry

The right of Warwick Merry to be identified as the author of this work has been asserted in accordance with the Copyright Amendment (Moral Rights) Act 2000.

All rights reserved. Without limiting the rights under copyright reserved above, no part of this publication may be reproduced, stored in a retrieval system or transmitted in any form or by any means, electronic, mechanical, photocopying, recording or otherwise without the prior written permission of the author.

National Library of Australia
Cataloguing-in-Publication Entry

Merry, Warwick, 1968-
Get More Inspiration: Unexpected ideas to help you achieve / Warwick Merry

ISBN 978-0-994-170200 (pbk)
ISBN 978-0-994-170217 (ebook)

Self-actualisation (Psychology)
Motivation (Psychology)
Success--Psychological aspects

158.1

Editor: Stephanie Jaehrling
Author Assistant: Lyn Prowse-Bishop
Designer: Sue Hamlet

# About the Author

Warwick Merry is referred to by his clients as Australia's best MC. He is also listed as the Voice of God on Wikipedia. He works with people and organisations to help them Get More Success in their business and their life.

An energetic, entertaining and engaging speaker, he is described as part Robin Williams and part Anthony Robbins. He also mentors business owners and senior managers to be the best they can be.

Warwick has presented in Germany, Denmark, Abu Dhabi, Sri Lanka, USA, New Zealand and Australia. He is also a keen singer with his vocal group Mood Swing and performs improvisation, stand-up comedy and theatrical productions.

He has been on the board of the National Speakers Association, served as their Victorian President and is active within the Global Speakers Federation sharing his knowledge and experience with other speakers.

Warwick is a Certified Speaking Professional, one of only 69 in Australia. This designation is recognised globally and is the highest level of accreditation in the speaking industry.

Warwick is based in Melbourne, Australia, and continues to write, speak and teach others how to Get More Success.

Find out more about his current projects at WarwickMerry.com

*For Sam.*
*You are truly perfect!*

# TABLE OF CONTENTS

About the Author ................................................................................ v
Steps to Success – START HERE! ...................................................... xv
What's the Theme? ............................................................................ 1
Yes, You Can Say No .......................................................................... 2
Who's Responsible? ........................................................................... 4
Is it Fun? ............................................................................................. 7
How to Get Up When You're Feeling Down ..................................... 8
Get out of Your Road! ...................................................................... 10
Get Closer by Moving Away ............................................................ 12
Don't Get Lost Following Your Intuition ......................................... 14
Check Your Facts ............................................................................. 16
Accidentally Famous ....................................................................... 17
What are You Listening to? ............................................................. 18
Christmas is for Giving .................................................................... 19
Go to the Edge ................................................................................. 20
I am Feeling ...................................................................................... 21
I Broke the Rules .............................................................................. 24
It's Hot .............................................................................................. 26
Don't Give Up ................................................................................... 28
Top 10 Tips for Life .......................................................................... 29
After the Crash ................................................................................ 30
What Will You Celebrate? ............................................................... 31
What Do You Want? ........................................................................ 32
Mum on a Motorbike ...................................................................... 33
What is Your Perspective? ............................................................... 34
What's in Your Head? ...................................................................... 35
Do You Have Piles? .......................................................................... 36
Do You Invest Well? ......................................................................... 37
Play With the Dog ............................................................................ 38
Gawk, Talk or Walk? ........................................................................ 40
What Would Spiderman Do? .......................................................... 41
It's the First Day! .............................................................................. 42
What is Your Plan? ........................................................................... 43

| | |
|---|---|
| What Motivates You? | 44 |
| How is Your Awareness? | 45 |
| How is Your Copying and Pasting? | 46 |
| Don't Just DO Something – Sit There! | 47 |
| Nothing Changes | 48 |
| What Inspires You? | 49 |
| Who is Driving? | 50 |
| Take it ALL! | 51 |
| What About Others? | 52 |
| What Does Johnny Cash Know? | 53 |
| Is it Too Hard? | 54 |
| Is it Good or Bad? | 55 |
| I'm Not Listening | 56 |
| He Touched Me! | 57 |
| What Sort of Impression Do You Make? | 58 |
| Big Impressions – Part II | 59 |
| Need More Adventure? | 60 |
| What Could You Do? | 62 |
| Should I be Committed? | 63 |
| Need a Challenge? | 64 |
| Do You Hear Voices? | 65 |
| Is it Fantasy or Planning? | 66 |
| Do You Look After Yourself? | 67 |
| Why Would You Tear Them Down? | 68 |
| Would You Like a Drink? | 69 |
| Are You Harry? | 70 |
| What were You Thinking? | 72 |
| What About Me? | 73 |
| Have You Got What You Need? | 74 |
| Have You Told Anyone? | 76 |
| Are They Eating out of Your Hand? | 78 |
| Have You Got Your Fat Bob? | 79 |
| Are You Sure it's Not Funny? | 80 |
| Do You Lead or Will You Get out of the Way? | 81 |
| How Come I am Not Perfect? | 84 |
| What is the Reality? | 85 |

| | |
|---|---|
| But Who are You Really? | 86 |
| Have You Got the Right Gear? | 88 |
| What Do You Want? | 89 |
| Who are You Selling to? | 90 |
| What Inspires You? | 91 |
| Are You Crazy? | 92 |
| Why Do You Do it? | 94 |
| How Do You Deal With it? | 95 |
| Are You Used to it? | 96 |
| Smile! | 97 |
| Can You Do it Again? | 98 |
| Is it Really You? | 99 |
| Is it OK to Give Compliments? | 100 |
| What About Me? | 102 |
| What are You Doing? | 103 |
| Will You Please Answer the Question? | 104 |
| Just Keep Swimming | 106 |
| What Can You Throw? | 107 |
| Why Have the Day off? | 108 |
| How Sharp is Your Saw? | 110 |
| How Hard is it? | 111 |
| Where is it from? | 112 |
| Is it Tragic or Magic? | 114 |
| What Do Little Old Ladies Know? | 116 |
| There is No Luck | 118 |
| What's the Risk? | 119 |
| How are Your Relationships? | 120 |
| The Phone Call | 121 |
| Is Your Reward Relevant? | 122 |
| Humans Can't See | 123 |
| What About this Weather? | 126 |
| What About the Little Guys? | 127 |
| Have You Exercised Your Slack Muscle? | 128 |
| What is Your Backup Plan? | 130 |
| How are Your Reflexes? | 132 |
| Is Your Body Where it Needs to be? | 133 |

| | |
|---|---|
| Are You Working Right? | 134 |
| How Do You Recover? | 135 |
| Can They Hear You? | 136 |
| What's Your Why? | 137 |
| Have You Broken the Habit? | 138 |
| Got Synergy? | 139 |
| Can You Make it Easy? | 140 |
| Are You Adding Value? | 142 |
| Are You Flexible? | 143 |
| Are You Protecting Your Assets? | 144 |
| Are You Trained? | 145 |
| How Good is Your Call to Action? | 146 |
| Do Your Systems Support You? | 147 |
| What Do You Want? | 148 |
| What Do You Think? | 149 |
| Things are Changing | 150 |
| Does it Hurt? | 151 |
| Have You Got a Card? | 152 |
| What Haven't You Said? | 153 |
| Do You Communicate Both Ways? | 154 |
| What's Happening? | 155 |
| Fanfare for the Common Man | 156 |
| How Big is Your Bite? | 157 |
| What are You Waiting for? | 158 |
| What Counts? | 159 |
| Got Leverage? | 160 |
| Your Skills Don't Count | 161 |
| It Will Not Work – My TEDx Story | 162 |
| What's Your Solution? | 163 |
| What's it for? | 164 |
| What Do I Get? | 165 |
| The Driver and the Dealer | 166 |
| What Do I Do Now? | 167 |
| Is That News? | 168 |
| What are You Talking About? | 169 |
| Are You on Focus? | 170 |

| | |
|---|---|
| There is No Escape! | 171 |
| Tough Leaders Create Tough Times | 172 |
| Get More Sales | 173 |
| What Do You Expect? | 174 |
| How was the Weekend? | 175 |
| Get More With Less | 176 |
| When Did You Last Celebrate? | 177 |
| How Positive is it? | 178 |
| Get More Patience | 179 |
| Free Trolley Ride | 180 |
| Take the Boat for a Spin | 181 |
| How to Stay Focussed | 182 |
| What if it's Too Late? | 183 |
| Just Relax! | 184 |
| What Can You Do? | 185 |
| Who Do You need? | 186 |
| Never Mind the Rain! | 187 |
| Be Unreasonable! | 188 |
| Going Shopping? | 189 |
| Good to be Exhausted | 190 |
| If You are Going, Go Hard! | 191 |
| Tell Me What You Want! | 192 |
| The Universe Provides | 193 |
| The Most Powerful Word | 194 |
| What's the First Thing? | 195 |
| Getting in Focus | 196 |
| Make Your Mind Up! | 197 |
| Are You Insane? | 198 |
| How is Your Perspective? | 199 |
| A Frightening Question! | 200 |
| How BIG is it? | 201 |
| You Have to Ask | 202 |
| What Do You Believe? | 203 |
| Time to Move | 204 |
| It's Not Safe! | 205 |
| Are You Happy Yet? | 206 |

| | |
|---|---|
| My Get Up and Go Has Got Up and Gone! | 207 |
| Let's Get Busy! | 208 |
| Acceptance Makes it Easier | 209 |
| How Much Extra is That? | 210 |
| What is Most Important? | 211 |
| How Smart are You? | 212 |
| Let's Have a Meeting! | 213 |
| How Attractive are You? | 214 |
| How Much Make-up is Enough? | 215 |
| Sometimes, it Takes Time! | 216 |
| What About You? | 217 |
| Are You Ready? | 218 |
| Is it Unacceptable? | 219 |
| What Will You Celebrate? | 220 |
| How Bizarre! | 221 |
| 12 Days of Christmas | 223 |
| A Risk or a Gamble? | 225 |
| Who Brought Your Success? | 226 |
| What Do You See? | 228 |
| It's Good | 229 |
| So What is it? | 230 |
| Who is it About? | 232 |
| Where is Your Tribe? | 233 |
| Will You Survive? | 234 |
| Don't be Subtle | 235 |
| Again, Again, Again | 236 |
| Is Your Email Worth $10,000? | 237 |
| The Most Productive Word in the World | 238 |
| What's Next? | 241 |

# Steps to Success – Start Here!

Let's make this easy!

The last thing I want to do is have you read this book, feel overwhelmed about what you haven't done or now need to do and get to the point where you put the book back on the shelf and ignore the fact that you started reading it.

I want the opposite to happen.

This book has been made so that you can flick it open on any page and get a burst of inspiration and some ideas on how you can Get More out of life – both at work and at home. It even has some direct action plans for you.

Too many of my clients and the people who hear me speak tell me that they have loads of business books – most of them are unread, some of them are partially read and a small percentage are read from cover to cover.

So to help you out, let me take the pressure off straight away. YOU DON'T HAVE TO READ THIS BOOK COMPLETELY. Whew … You can relax now.

As mentioned above, I have created this book as a flicker. To make it even easier to get value out of your investment of time and money in this book, I have created the Six Steps to Success. The good news is that they apply not only to this book, but other resources you may already have.

Good luck with all your endeavours and I trust this book will help you get there. If I can help you at all, please contact me via my website WarwickMerry.com

And now, the steps you need!

# SIX STEPS TO SUCCESS

1. **Pace yourself**

   There is no rush to finish this book or complete every exercise in it all at once, so pace yourself. You have many elements in your life. It is up to you to make sure they all get enough attention.

   Having said that you MUST pay this book some attention. Why not set yourself a schedule of 30 minutes a week to flick to a few entries and then put into action the ideas involved. Surely you have 30 minutes a week available, even if it means you get up a little earlier one day.

2. **Enjoy the journey**

   Have fun with this. You will be amazed at the ideas and the benefits you, your family, your colleagues and your workplace will receive once you start applying the ideas within – as well as the ideas you get after being inspired by this book.

   It is important to be focussed on the outcome you are working towards, but enjoy the process that gets you there. Too often people achieve a goal that they had been focussing on and then think "Is that it?" Enjoy every moment as you go

3. **Revisit this resource regularly**

   It is tempting to read a book or resource, think "That's awesome" and then get on with life never referring to it again. The ideas and inspiration in this book are timeless. The examples and experiences used may date but the principles and concepts won't.

   Revisiting the book and repeating some of the exercises will continue to bring you value, so do it.

4. **Take action**

   > Action is the magic word,
   > Not words are the magic action.

   Having this book on your shelf, next to your bed, in your carry case or even on your desk will do nothing but collect dust. Reading the book, nodding at the good ideas, laughing at the funny bits, agreeing with the principles or thinking one of your team will benefit from that reading does NOTHING!

To get any return from your investment of time and money in reading this book YOU MUST TAKE ACTION.

Do anything. Write an action plan, brainstorm ideas, implement a concept, have a discussion about it, change your habit for a day, shift your perspective – do anything.

Don't be scared of making a mistake either. Know that when you make mistakes, you are one step closer to success. Don't let them stop you from continuing to implement new ideas.

In all elements of business and life, it is action that will generate results.

## 5. Get others involved

One of the best ways to ensure that you take some action is to have an accountability partner. It is as simple as letting a colleague, partner, child, friend, coach or me know that you are going to do something and ask for an accountability call/conversation in a week or two to see how it is going.

Knowing that you will have this accountability call will give you additional motivation to take action. You may not complete it, but at the very least you will want to start.

If you find this book useful, why not share it with others or suggest they get their own copy? They can get a copy at GetMoreInspiration.com

## 6. Reward yourself

> **When celebrating success becomes a habit success becomes a habit.**

Too often we move from one success on to the next process. Frequently smaller successes are not even acknowledged.

When you achieve something, celebrate it. You don't have to spend loads of money, but do something commensurate with the value of the achievement.

If you achieve a massive sale, buy yourself something you usually wouldn't as a treat. If you change a habit, celebrate by having a pleasant experience (it may be locking the kids out of the bathroom and having a relaxing bath or just spending an hour in nature).

We are too often our own worst enemy. It is time for that to stop. Be your own cheerleader and celebrate your success and those around you.

All of a sudden, you will find you have so much to celebrate.

# What's the Theme?

Happy New Year!

I hope that this year is full of success, fun and happiness.

Did you make a new year's resolution? I think new year's resolutions are too hard. Too many things to remember, too easy to get side-tracked, too easy to go back to old habits, too similar to last year's resolutions (or is that revolutions), and too easy to simply lose interest.

So for this year, I am having a theme. It is something in addition to the goals of my business and my personal goals, but it is the essence of my focus for the year. It is something to keep me on track and progressing. It is one simple statement; in fact it is three simple words. It's easy to remember, easy to focus on and easy to adjust my course when I stray.

My theme for this year is:

**Make an impact!**

What's yours?

**My theme for the next year is:**
_____
_____
_____
_____
_____
_____
_____

# Yes, You Can Say No

This comes up time and time again in my workshops, with my coaching/mentoring clients and even with my friends. So I wanted to clarify this.

It is okay to say no.

You may not feel that way; you may feel that if you don't do it no one else will. Or maybe you can't say no because you "should" say yes. You have a rule that family members, friends, colleagues, bosses, workers "SHOULD" perform in a certain way.

From my own bitter experience, I have found out that saying yes all the time is great for everyone else, but really bad for me! They get everything they want and I get exhausted and resentful. But the real kicker is that they want you to say no. They may not think it, but they do.

Your boss will continue to ask you to do things and when you are at full capacity, they want you to say no. Your friends will keep asking for favours and expect that if you can't do it, that you say no. It may not seem it at the time but they would much prefer you to say no upfront than get to their deadline and have you inform them that because you have too much on you couldn't do it. Your family would much prefer you to say that you don't want to go along to the family trip versus whinging and moaning about it for months afterwards.

Yes, the short term is painful. Letting people know that you can't or won't do, say or be what they want is challenging. But the long-term payoff is so worthwhile. Once you have established the boundaries of what you will and won't do, each party has a far better understanding of each other. There are fewer assumptions and expectations and fewer opportunities for mixed messages.

So start practising today! What do you need to say no to? How can you say no respectfully and with care? Maybe you could start with smaller things and work your way up once your no muscle has had a bit of a workout?

But don't forget to practise the other side of the equation also! If someone says no to you, don't hassle them or berate them. Allow them the courtesy of saying what they need to for them. As we know, saying no is not always easy, but it is always worthwhile.

**Things I need to say no to:**

# Who's Responsible?

There has been a lot said about clean feeds and internet filters that has come across my radar.

In summary, the Australian Government wants to filter the internet so that "naughty" sites will not be accessible. Different community groups and user communities have been expressing their opinions for and against the ideas. There are technology issues such as any filter is quickly made redundant by the people it was supposed to protect (the same way Dad used to bring me the headache drug bottle with a child-proof lid because he couldn't open it and I could – I was in primary school!). Filtering will slow the internet down – the technology tests have proven it but common sense does too. Look at any pool filter and you will see the water does not flow freely; it has to be pumped or sucked through. Why should the internet be any different?

There are issues in administering the filter. Who decides what is blacklisted and what is not? Who has input to the decision-making? What guidelines will be used? Who creates the guidelines?

There are issues in the ethics of the internet filter. Should this be done? Does it impact our free speech? Is it for the greater good? An extreme case of this can be seen in the film, Serenity. For the good of the whole, the government meddles and causes a disaster. I know it is fiction, but how does the meddling start?

The thing that gets me is not whether the government should or should not have an internet filter, but why are they getting involved?

Is it because parents are too lazy to do it for themselves?

Many teacher friends of mine comment on how parents expect the teacher and school to teach EVERYTHING to the student. Not just reading, writing and arithmetic, but manners, ethics, social behaviours and a myriad of other skills. Granted the internet and technology are rapidly changing and it is hard to keep up, but surely it can't be too difficult to have them use the internet in a room where they can be supervised or limited in the number of hours they are on the internet?

Heaven forbid that parents have a discussion with the child about pitfalls of the internet! Next thing you know people will expect parents to listen to their own children read aloud to them!

The bigger issue that I see happening is one of responsibility. It is becoming rarer than ever in our society. Yet the people who take responsibility for their actions and their lack of actions are the ones that move ahead in their life. They are not looking for an easy way out, a person to blame, someone to handpass the problem to. They look at what is their part in this issue.

In my life and in my presentations, I share with people what I call the "two killer questions".

They are:

> What is my part in this?
> What can I do differently?

It means that as an individual I can look at "What is my responsibility?" So with Clean Feed and internet filters, what is it that I want for my kids, myself or my workplace? Has this situation come about due to some action or inaction on my part?

Maybe I have no part in the current situation but I want it to be different. What action must I take? Do I need to supervise people, limit certain sites in the workplace, communicate an internet policy, write to the government and let them know my wishes?

Responsibility means that I have the ability to respond. I can take action to get the results I am after.

Beyond the internet filters, beyond the clean feed, beyond raising a family, but in life as a whole, I strongly urge you to take FULL responsibility. It doesn't mean you have to do everything; you can ask for help (I am here if you need me!), but do take responsibility for your choices, your actions and your lack of actions.

Remember the two killer questions.

Once you have done that, it's easy!

---

**The killer questions**

## What's my part in this?

_____
_____
_____
_____
_____
_____

## What can I do differently?

_____
_____
_____
_____
_____
_____

# Is it Fun?

One of the most energy-draining aspects of work is seriousness.

Don't get me wrong, there is a time and place to be serious, but it seems that it is becoming ALL the time and EVERY place!

How many times have you been part of:

- Meetings that have just dragged on while someone was waffling about the importance of so-and-so and you could tell that NO ONE was listening?
- Sales presentations where the salesperson was so serious, it turned you off their product?
- Conversations with colleagues who sounded like they were running down a checklist of things to say?

The Minister of Fun at a conference I was at had one simple rule. It is a rule I like more and more each day.

"If it's not fun, don't do it. If you have to do it, make it fun."

That doesn't mean that you make everything an opportunity for stand-up comedy. You don't want to be disruptive; you simply want to make it fun.

So are you having fun yet?

---

**Where do I need to add more fun?**

_____
_____
_____
_____
_____

# How to Get Up When You're Feeling Down

Ever had those moments?

Everything seems to be cruising along nicely. Your relationship is good (if not getting better and better), friends are good (still get invites to go out), hobbies are good (love cruising on the motorbike or doing what you do), health is good (could always do more exercise and eat less but on the whole it's good), work is good (love what you do and do what you love), weather is good (sunny day after a bit of rain) so basically, life is good!

Then it hits! Wham! You feel like crap!

It has no obvious source or reason, you just feel bad. Self-doubt kicks in and your self-esteem crumbles little by little. Arrrrrrgghhhh!!

Ever had one of those moments?

We all do. They will pass. The secret is to look at ways to help them pass faster. Here are a few that my clients have found very successful:

**Music** – play music that works for you, something that makes you feel more powerful.

**Exercise** – any form of exercise will help endorphins start flowing and give you some of nature's "happy juice".

**Location** – change your physical location. It could be just going outside; it may be going to the beach – something that gives you a different perspective.

**Talk** – chat with a friend or colleague about what is happening for you and more importantly, what is happening for them. It takes the obsession off ourselves and turns it into caring for others.

Write – ink what you think. This will get the never-ending tape out of your head and onto paper. By the way, typing doesn't count; the physical act of writing is required.

There are plenty of other ways to get a sense of reality and move through the downer. Work out what is best for you and have it on standby for when these times hit.

If nothing else, follow the words of the late great James Brown:

"Get up, get on up!"

**Action plan for when I need to fire up:**

# GET OUT OF YOUR ROAD!

I have been Twittering with friends about the joys of Australia. They are both from the USA and said they would love to visit one day.

It got me thinking.

So many people get in their own roads for doing things. Rather than focussing on reasons why they can do something, they look for reasons why they can't:

- It's too far
- I don't know anyone there
- What would I do?
- Where would I stay?
- They speak funny
- I don't think I can afford it
- I don't want to go by myself
- What if I need to get back in a hurry?
- I don't like flying

… The list goes on!

That is not just for a frivolous trip halfway around the world. I have also heard:

- What about the economic crisis?
- I've never done that before
- I have other responsibilities
- You can't be spiritual and rich at the same time
- People wouldn't understand
- It's too hot
- It's too cold
- It's too hard
- It's too easy

- I could never do that
- People will laugh
- What will my husband/wife/kids/parents/friends/counsellor /postman think?

… And the list goes on.

Get out of your own road! If you really want it, go for it. Go for it with everything you have. Don't let what you can't do get in the road of what you can do.

So what are the reasons you WILL be doing what you have always dreamed of?

**What do I really want and what is stopping me?**
_____
_____
_____
_____
_____
_____
_____
_____
_____
_____
_____
_____
_____
_____
_____

# Get Closer by Moving Away

Web 2.0 amazes me. I mean, not like a magician making your aunt levitate, but in its appeal to the masses. In one way it is drawing us closer together, but in another it seems we are moving further and further apart. We are getting closer by moving away.

Let me explain.

As a country lad (that's why I speak slowly!) I grew up in a town of about 2,000 people. We didn't have many people to speak to so you spoke to everyone. Everyone knew what everyone else was doing. There was even the local paper (that came out once a week), which updated you if you didn't know.

Things are different in the city. You are surrounded by people and are always alone. People don't talk to their neighbours. We rarely acknowledge passers-by. Technology has made it even worse. Protected by the cocoon of our iPod or MP3 player we blissfully ignore the rest of the world. We sit behind our computers or play our video games minimising human contact.

In fact, we have disconnected so much that we are challenged in communicating difficult news. We end a relationship via text, resign from our job via email, have sick days via text or leave voicemail messages so we don't have to face the person we are talking to.

Along comes Web 2.0. (or is it now Web 3.9?)

All this time we are alone builds our desire to genuinely connect – but we can't handle the rejection if it doesn't work. The technology can act as a great barrier and we can connect without risk. You can Tweet someone on the other side of the world, have a couple of short 140-character jokes and all is good. You can post things on Facebook, MySpace and your blog to let the world know what you think (hey I have two blogs – double the nerd!).

You can link with people on Facebook and LinkedIn. You may even have thousands of connections, friends, affiliates, followers, without realising it is more than the population of my hometown! You may even break out of the 140-character restriction and email your new friend.

Want to surprise someone? Offer to meet them in person! If they agree to meet, you will find one thing. To be more precise, I found one thing. People disclose more via technology than face-to-face. We don't like putting ourselves at risk. We can't delete the post, change the blog content or take back what we said when we are talking face-to-face.

My challenge and one that I issue to you is to be authentic. Just be you. People will love it and will love (or at least like a lot) you for doing it.

The other challenge is to talk to your neighbours. Tweet them in real life. Chat to the people on the train. People down the street. You don't have to be deep and meaningful, but while technology is great, NOTHING beats human connection!

**People I need to meet face-to-face:**
_____
_____
_____
_____
_____
_____
_____
_____
_____

# Don't Get Lost Following Your Intuition

There has been a lot written over the years about following your intuition. Many people have been on some weird, wacky and wonderful journeys over time. But while a lot of writing, blogging, texting, reading and listening has been done, I still get asked time and time again "How do I follow my intuition?" What I propose is not THE answer, more it is AN answer. It works for me. Give it a try because it may work for you too!

First up, what is your intuition? Some think it is your subconscious talking to you, some say it is a gut feel and others talk about laws of attraction suggesting a course of action. Here is how I see it.

For those of you who know me you will know that I am a hippy in a suit. I have worked in the corporate world for 20 years and I have a strong spiritual life as well. By spiritual I don't mean religion, as they are different. In my life I have a Higher Power who I call God. You may call it fate, destiny, the angels, the universe, Buddha, Christ, the Force – I don't care. What you call it is your decision. I believe because my life is better for it and it gives me strength.

How this relates to intuition is this. I believe that prayer is when I talk with God and meditation is when God talks to me. I have asked God many times to just send me an email, a text or even a Twitter message as they are clear, but God doesn't. God prefers to communicate in a different manner, God does it via my intuition.

While I meditate to listen, I also keep the channel open by following my intuition.

When I first became aware of my intuition, I found I ignored it. I even heard myself say later, "If only I had done what I thought I should". After a while, making mistakes gets boring! So rather than saying "if only" when it didn't work, I started listening. For me, my intuition is like a muscle. The more I use it, the stronger it gets. It helps me see things I would have missed, do things I would not have done and sense opportunities that would have passed me by.

So, when you are thinking "How do I follow my intuition?", start by listening. The voice or sense will be there. It may be faint, but it will be there. It is a slow but steady feeling that a certain course of action is the best one for you to take. It is not an overwhelming sense of urgency but a solid and constant force for positive results in you and your life.

My coaching/mentor clients sometimes say that they can't hear it. That's when you fake it 'til you make it. Ask yourself the question, if you could hear your intuition, what would it say – and then do that! Act as if and you will reap the rewards.

The best thing is that there is no wrong answer. You are the only one who can hear your intuition. Act with the best intent and you can't go wrong!

**What does my intuition say to me?**
_____
_____
_____
_____
_____
_____
_____
_____
_____
_____

# Check Your Facts

I don't know about you, but sometimes I get all fired up about what I think and not what I know. Let me explain.

Out the front of our house were ten large pine trees. The previous owner planted them about 15 years ago thinking they would become a nice 1.2 metre (4 foot) hedge. Being trees rather than shrubs, they grew (and grew and grew and grew) and now ended up about 6 metres (20 feet) high and skilfully blocked all of the sunshine that could be shining into our house.

When discussing getting them cut down my gorgeous wife and I guessed it was going to cost about $5,000-$10,000 based on an old quote from a few years ago. Being a little financially conservative, naturally I allowed more for the $10,000 than the $5,000. So we didn't worry about them. They were not a priority and we could get them cut down at a later date.

I finally decided to find out how much it would cost to get them removed. I was pleased to find out it was only $2,500 to get all the trees and stumps removed. So we did.

How many times have you or your company made decisions without the readily and easily available facts? Guesses, ideas, feelings, vibes, intuition and plucking it out of the air cannot compete with facts. Don't get me wrong, sometimes these things are good enough or even essential, but sometimes it is the facts that make the difference.

So, my challenge to you is to channel your inner Joe Friday (from Dragnet) and ask for "just the facts".

I guarantee it will make your decisions a lot more clear-cut.

# Accidentally Famous

You never know who reads your site, blog, twitter, Facebook or whatever else you do.

While "famous" is a bit of a stretch, I was pleased to find out that my ex-poodle was referred to on an English TV series. He was a chocolate toy poodle and his name was Burma. He was so full of energy and life but unfortunately he burst a disc in his back and I had to have him put down – a very difficult and heart-wrenching decision.

Stephen Fry was the host of a BBC program called Quite Interesting where they would chat about obscure facts and look for funny answers to challenging questions. After talking about the country Burma and getting ready to go to the ad break, Stephen looked to camera and said:

> Actually, interestingly, while double-checking this information on etiquette and Burma on the internet, we came up with the extraordinary information that it's considered polite to express joy by eating snow and to send unwanted guests away by biting their leg and normal behaviour to wipe your mouth on the sofa. This is actually true, the researchers were writing this down with great excitement about Burma, only to discover in the end that Burma turned out to be the name of a poodle belonging to the author of the website.

The point is – yes, there is a point – you never know who will see what you write and where it will be. That page of my old website is long gone, it went with Burma, but it had an impact!

What sort of impact will you have?

# WHAT ARE YOU LISTENING TO?

What are you listening to right now?

Not what is on the radio, not what is on TV, not what others are saying, but what is it that is in your head? What is the endless loop of self-talk saying?

So many people hear "You probably won't get that sale", "You won't look very good in that outfit", "Who are you trying to kid with that idea", "Better be scared of where the economy is heading", and a vast array of other negative things.

STOP IT!!

Your thoughts become your words.
Your words become your actions.
Your actions become your habits.
Your habits become your beliefs and your beliefs set your destiny.

Choose the positive thoughts. Use words that show those thoughts. Take action to reflect your words and you will ensure your habits, beliefs and destiny are on the course to success.

So ... what are you listening to now?

**What positive thoughts can I tell myself?**
_____
_____
_____
_____
_____

# Christmas is for Giving

As I was thinking about Christmas (one of my favourite times of the year), I considered what I have been told as a kid, that Christmas is for giving. It was only when I wrote that sentence down that I noticed the truth of it.

"Christmas is for giving" or possibly "Christmas is forgiving".

What a cool thing! Christmas is forgiving. What a gift to give yourself and others this year! Forgiveness! Who are some of the people and institutions you could give the gift of forgiveness to?

**Yourself** – Is there anything you blame yourself for that you could now let go of?

**Your family** – Do you still hold any grudges for things that your family members said, did, didn't say or didn't do?

**Your friends** – Do you have any friends you need to forgive?

**Institutions** – Are there any companies (banks, post offices, utility supplier, ISPs, online services and so on) who have crapped you off this year that you need to forgive?

You know the best thing about forgiveness? You are the one that benefits the most. By forgiving others you get freedom from baggage that you have been carrying around all this time. You get to lighten your load and focus on being the real you, not someone driven crazy by the weird and wonderful people in your life.

Give it a try! You may be surprised at the results and you don't even have to use giftwrapping!

# Go to the Edge

A while ago I entered the Triple J Raw Comedy Competition.

I don't mind confessing that I was a little scared! I like to think I am a little funny and that I keep people amused at parties, but being on stage in the spotlight is a little different.

You may also know that I am a professional speaker so being in front of people is not a new experience for me. But there is a huge difference between cracking a few jokes during a one-hour session and making people laugh constantly for five minutes.

Five minutes! It is not long but it can seem like a lifetime. I had a routine written and I was pretty confident (to be honest I was a bit too confident!) and then I performed it in front of ten friends at a comedy writing workshop.

Ouch! It wasn't that good. So I have spent a lot of time writing and rewriting my five minutes of comedy.

I have thought about doing this for ages. There is no reason for me to do this other than to go to the edge and peer over. I don't want to fail. I want to be funny! In fact, to be completely honest, I want to get to the next round. For years I have avoided this but I can't do it anymore.

What about you? What edge do you need to go to?

**The edge I need to go to:**

_____
_____
_____
_____

# I am Feeling

As a speaker I address audiences from five to 5,000 and feel incredibly comfortable in doing so. In fact, the bigger the audience the better.

It was really strange to be in a dingy dark room at the back of an iconic Melbourne hotel with about 120-150 people in the audience and be really nervous. After 30 seconds on stage, I was able to relax a bit and then proceeded. So even though I haven't been nervous like that for quite a while, it passed quickly.

What didn't pass quickly were my other feelings!

I am a student of personal development and the New Age learning.

Manifesting, Law of Attraction, Power of Positive Thinking and lots of other fun hippy trippy stuff. After a humble assessment of my comedy skill I thought that there was a fair chance I may progress to the second round. When I was doing my preparation I was focussed on performing well enough to get to the second round.

I was fortunate to be part of a pre-heat comedy workshop and after seeing others my confidence of getting to the second round was boosted.

On the day that 31 people gave their performances of five minutes each, six of them were to progress to the next round. After the level of laughs I got and the positive feedback from honest friends, I was confident that the second round would manifest into reality for me.

As I watched more and more of the Raw Comedy entrants I could honestly say that there were about two or three who were significantly better than me and others that were close. The leader of the comedy workshop had a chat with me at half-time and said in his opinion I had a strong chance of getting through.

When the six entrants going through to the next round were announced, my name wasn't one of them. Some of the people who did get through didn't seem to be as funny as me or have as good a crowd response as I did. But comedy is a funny thing – not funny "ha ha" but funny strange. What appealed to the judges was different to what appealed to me.

My friends and my own mind kicked in:

> "You gave it your best shot."
> "Others would not have done this."
> "The judges got it wrong – we thought you were great."
> "There is always next year."
> "It wasn't meant to be."

I tried to be philosophical. I looked for the positive. I sent positive vibes to the winners.

I was as pissed off as hell!

Well, maybe not that much but I was very disappointed. This was where the feelings were kicking in. I know about acceptance, moving forward, letting go of disappointment, blessing others who achieve what you want – but I still had feelings. Sometimes in the New Age writings it seems like they think I am Buddha. I am not that nice!

So I felt pissed off for a couple of hours. It was great. I got in there and really wallowed in it. I felt the feelings and they passed.

They no longer hold me back. I can be authentic and not pretend I am something I am not. I wasn't unpleasant, in fact I genuinely congratulated the others, but I allowed myself to feel the feelings.

Some well-intentioned people around me tried to shut the feelings down but I knew what was right for me.

What about you? What is right for you? How do you process your feelings?

They say that the quickest way around is through. If you want to be free of the damage your feelings can cause to you and those you love (or even just your work colleagues), don't squash the feelings down. Feel them. Process them. Have a tantrum if you need to (just make sure it is in an appropriate place). Once the feeling has gone you are free to do what you know you must.

Me ... I am now looking around for open mic nights at the many Melbourne comedy clubs. I won't let one little setback get in my road – no matter how disappointing!

**What feelings do I need to feel so they pass?**

# I Broke the Rules

I knew the rules but didn't meet them.

It still pissed me off!!

I was flying to my band camp (Summer Song) and I was excited! I had a 7.30 flight and was flying Jetstar. For those who don't know, Jetstar is one of Australia's low cost airlines – effectively a bus with wings. They have a policy that check-in closes 30 minutes before the flight takes off and if you miss check-in, you miss your flight.

I was clever – I checked in from home using web check-in. All I had to do was check my bag and I was good to go. So on Thursday morning I got up early, woke my gorgeous wife (who was my chauffer for the day) and headed off to the airport.

Unfortunately traffic was a little tight, but no worries, because my baggage was in a carry-on bag so if I was late I would just carry it on. I got there at 7.00 am, joined the queue to check bags at 7.02 am and spoke to the check-in person at 7.04 am. He informed me that baggage was closed. "No worries", I said, "I'll just carry it on". He said it was a little heavy and I had to see the service desk.

There I was waiting in line to see the service desk dude, getting concerned about how close it was to the flight. When the service desk dude finished with his customer I mentioned to him (because I was four people back in the queue) that I was concerned I would miss my flight. Then he said I had been taken off the flight and I would have to reschedule.

That's when I felt like a four-year-old in a lolly shop with no money. Adrenalin surged, I was going to start shouting and blame Jetstar. They would be sorry and I would never fly with them again. I would tweet everyone and … it was all my fault.

I knew the rules and I didn't stick by them. I was late to check-in. Jetstar are known for their strict adherence to this policy. I had joked with a friend the week before about how she missed her flight for last year's camp.

I didn't add a buffer. When planning anything I always like to add a buffer for when things are not perfect. Traffic was heavier than I thought and five minutes delay cost me.

I was too heavy. My baggage was 3 kg too heavy for carry on. I knew there were limits and I know Jetstar is strict. Next time I will pack differently.

I didn't blow up and blame them for all of my woes. I still have issues with their policies, but I knew their policies and didn't follow them.

The best thing I did was take responsibility for my actions. My fault and no one else's.

So there I was at the airport, one day later, $70 poorer and rescheduling my trip.

Where do you need to take responsibility?

**I need to take responsibility:**
_____
_____
_____
_____
_____
_____
_____
_____
_____

# IT'S HOT

Sometimes it gets hot. Damn hot. Heatwaves with multiple days over 40 °C (about 105 °F).

Who cares?

Fair question. Many parts of the world have temperatures higher than this all the time (hello Middle East), but they don't moan like we do. At the very least people blog about it. Twitter is rife with it. The newspapers all have the delightful headline "SCORCHER" – or something equally as witty. Tennis commentators waffle on for ages about it. Radio commentators all go on about it also.

What can you do?

The answer is – nothing. The weather is the rare topic that we talk about all the time and can do nothing about. Whatever you mention about it, someone has it better and someone has it worse. Tweets of "it's hot" were countered with "at least you don't have an ice storm like we do".

Sometimes just talking about it makes it worse. While it is hard not to talk about it, it will still be hot when your conversation has ended. All you can do is make yourself as comfortable as possible (popular ideas are to go to an air-conditioned cinema or the beach) and get on with life.

What else is like that?

How many times in business or life does this situation occur? There is always something that you can bitch and moan about and all it gets you is more distressed, even more unhappy and more focussed on something you can do nothing about. It could be your family, a health affliction, someone's behaviour or even the weather!

How will you deal with it?

I like the two killer questions:

- What's my part in this?
- What can I do differently?

They will always generate an answer that lets me take responsibility for my situation and move on.

**How will I take responsibility for my situation?**

# Don't Give Up

There are always times when we are challenged and want to give up. Maybe not give up, but let things slide. Go for an easier, softer option.

For me, there are times when my focus has to be don't give up! Or as good friends of mine say, "Don't quit before the miracle happens".

For you, what is happening in your life that needs you to persist just that little bit longer? What do you need to do to let go of past performance, what you may have previously said or done and focus on the right here and right now? What will you do to keep applying yourself and focus on the desired outcome?

Calvin Coolidge (30th President of the USA) has been often quoted saying:

> Nothing in the world can take the place of persistence. Talent will not; nothing is more common than unsuccessful men with talent. Genius will not; unrewarded genius is almost a proverb. Education will not; the world is full of educated derelicts. Persistence and determination alone are omnipotent. The slogan 'Press on' has solved and always will solve the problems of the human race.

But I am more a fan of the Captain from Galaxy Quest.

**"Never give up. Never surrender!"**

# Top 10 Tips for Life

1. Stay out of trouble that you can easily avoid.
2. No matter how high you go, you can always aim for greater heights.
3. Whatever you are doing, maintain your focus.
4. We all get busy, but you need to find time for exercise to maintain your health.
5. You are not alone in the world so practise teamwork because you can't do everything.
6. Trust your partner to watch your back. Being able to trust is as important as having someone to trust.
7. You never know when the rainy day will hit. You need to make sure you put a little aside to give you protection.
8. Take time to rest. You will need to restore your energy for all your adventures.
9. Always remember to smile. You may find yourself in a strange position with strange people and a smile will always help.
10. No matter what anyone says, nothing is impossible!

# After the Crash

I sometimes watch the Melbourne Grand Prix. A day of noise, colour, excitement, people and crashes. So many crashes. So many expensive, jaw-crunching, bowel-clenching crashes.

What do you think that the driver would say after the crash: "Well that's it. I can't race anymore"? I doubt it.

I suspect the whole team will ask, "What did we do wrong? What can we do better or different? What can we learn from this?"

That sounds like a winning thing to do. Why then as individuals do we make mistakes and then think we can NEVER do that thing again? Or berate ourselves so much over minor incidents?

Let's learn from the pros and ask ourselves:

- What did I do wrong?
- What can I do better or different?
- What can I learn from this?

Then get back in the driver's seat, buckle up and have another go!

**What do I need to have "another go" at?**
_____
_____
_____
_____
_____
_____

# What Will You Celebrate?

I find grand finals of elite sport fascinating!

At the end of the game there are a lot of celebrations by the victors and their supporters. It is the end of a huge amount of effort over the year, a lot of training, focus and sacrifice for their goal. The team that didn't win would have put in the same amount of effort, focus and sacrifice – but they are not celebrating.

Don't forget how hard it is to ALMOST reach your goals. It is easy to get in to blame mode (what the coach did or didn't do), to punish mode (I am not supporting them next year) or give up mode (that's it – I no longer care about the game!).

We do the same with our own goals. We may get 98% of the way there and not quite achieve them. That is no reason to blame, punish or give up! It is a reason to review what worked and what didn't. Look at what you can do to improve and also a reason to celebrate. I believe that if you make celebrating success a habit, success becomes a habit. Don't focus on the 2% you didn't achieve, focus on the great things you have achieved. (Some days that can be just turning up to work!)

**Things I need to celebrate:**
_____
_____
_____
_____
_____
_____

# WHAT DO YOU WANT?

I am one of those people who is "a bit slow catchin' on". As I said to my gorgeous wife when we first got together, "I don't do subtle". It is the same with my coaching clients. I advise them that they are not to suggest, imply, hint, wish, hope or be subtle about what they want or need. If you are subtle or only hinting, you could talk for days about something and I may not get what you are after.

The same can be said for life in general. If you want something, ask for it. The classic bible quote of "Ask and it shall be given unto you" may not always be accurate but it works better than just wishing for something.

How many discounts are you missing out on because you don't ask for it? How much special treatment do you miss because you never ask?

I was once travelling and stopped at a hotel. When booking in I asked how much was the room. I asked was there a corporate rate, to which the attendant said yes and quoted the price, which was about 20% cheaper. When I asked how I could get the corporate rate, she said, "You just have to ask for it". Naturally I asked for it!

What are you missing out on because you don't ask for it?

**What do I need to ask for?**
_____
_____
_____
_____
_____
_____

# Mum on a Motorbike

I gave my mum a lift home from the city.

There is nothing unusual about that. People do it all the time. But my mum lives in a sleepy town with a population of about 2,000 and traffic is not usually that busy. She was visiting me in Melbourne, population about four million and peak hour is … well … messy at times! Not only that, but I ride a motorbike. Granted, it is a big one, but it means you are much closer to the large semi-trailers than you are when in the car.

So there we were zooming home on the bike, me on the front hoping everyone would know I had my mum on the back so they should give way, and my septuagenarian mum on the back grinning like a Cheshire cat. She had a ball! In fact, she liked it so much that after we got home, we got back on the bike and went for another ride to the pub for dinner.

As much as I like bragging about my mum, the point of this is don't let invisible boundaries stop you from doing things. When I mentioned to people I was giving mum a lift home many people on my client site said things like: "Ooo … is that a good idea?", "Your mum? Really?" Even other motorbike riders were saying "I am not sure I would do that". At what age do you get "too old" to do things? Too mature, too tall, too many responsibilities, too serious, too risky, too (insert relevant word here)?

Life is to be lived. Don't let what others think hold you back.

**What holds me back?**
_____
_____
_____

# What is Your Perspective?

Perspective can have such a significant impact on how we see a situation.

I live in Melbourne where we have trams as a form of public transport. When I am in a tram, I want all the cars and pedestrians to get out of my way because they slow me down and I just want to keep moving. When I am in a car, I want the tram to go away because I have to stop more, the traffic is slower and pedestrians just step out onto the road – they slow me down and I just want to keep moving. When I am a pedestrian, I want all traffic (be they car, bus, tram, motorbike or pushbike) to get out of my way because they don't consider me and get in my way – they slow me down and I just want to keep moving.

When I shift my perspective, my journey becomes more pleasant.

When I'm in my car, if I recall how I feel when I'm on the tram or a pedestrian, I become more considerate. The same thing happens when I'm a pedestrian or on the tram considering how I feel when I am on the other modes of transport. My situation is still the same, but a shift in perspective makes the situation more pleasant and somehow it seems quicker and less draining.

What about you? What situation do you need to change your perspective on? Is it dealing with your kids, your partner, your boss, your colleagues, your pets, that guy at the train station, the person selling *Big Issue* magazines, or maybe it is how you relate to yourself? What is your perspective?

# WHAT'S IN YOUR HEAD?

It seems to me that one of the worst voices we listen to is that one that is in our head. What do you hear when someone gives you feedback?

If someone is giving constructive criticism do you jump to, "Typical, I've stuffed up again"?

If someone gives you a compliment do you hear, "They're just saying that"?

When you achieve fantastic results do you hear, "But I could have done better"?

The voice does not serve you well. It can often sound like a parent, an old teacher, a sibling or a jealous rival. You are best often to ignore or silence the voice. When the voice kicks in, tell yourself: "That is NOT what they are saying" and listen to what the feedback actually is.

When someone is giving you feedback the best thing to do is accept it. You may not agree with it, but there will be value in it. To know someone thinks you have done well, or to find ways you can improve what you are doing, or to accept that you are not perfect but you are improving is a far more valuable way to deal with this situation.

So what is that voice saying now?

**How will I accept my next compliment?**

_____
_____
_____
_____

# Do You Have Piles?

Are you one of these people with piles?

What I mean is piles of paper on your desk, the window sill, the floor, your secretary's desk? Maybe you even have them on the bench at home or in your home office? You know the piles I am talking about. They are the "I'll do that later" piles.

These piles drain your energy. Just looking at them exhausts you.

Have you ever turned up to work, looked at your desk and then left it in search of the coffee you need to get you started? You HAVE to get rid of your piles.

Here are some easy ways:

- Do it – so often we spend more energy putting something off than actually doing it.
- Dump it – you may be delaying it because you are not going to do it; just throw it away. My theory is "when in doubt, chuck it out".
- Delegate it – maybe someone else is better off doing this one for you.
- Deposit it – your pile may just need filing or archiving.
- Diarise it – now may not be the best time to deal with a pile, so diarise an appointment with yourself when you will do it, and file the pile in your pending area until you need it.

Once you have dealt with your physical piles, what about your virtual piles? We call it email!

# Do You Invest Well?

It occurs to me that successful people invest well. They look at all the options available and put their hard-earned cash where they will get the best return.

Do you invest well?

Successful people dabble a bit in shares, some in options, a bit in property, maybe some bonds, but that is not their most significant investment. They get returns there but not like their best investment.

Do you invest well?

After doing some research, I found the best investment they make is the one in themselves! It is not always cash either. Sometimes it is in time too. Time to rest, time to recreate themselves, time to learn new ways or time to recharge their energy.

Do you invest well?

Until recently I had not invested in my own learning for a while. I went to a course and had the opportunity to learn new ideas, refresh old learning, meet new associates, and invest more in myself. It was the best investment I have made in some time.

Do you invest well?

What investment will you make in yourself? Anything that grows you and your knowledge can only be described as investing well!

# Play With the Dog

My gorgeous wife and I had a delightful, extravagant meal of fish and chips on the beach. I am sure you don't care, but I saw something that made me think.

A young woman took her dog to the beach for a walk and a play. As she got to the beach I noticed she was on the mobile.

The dog was running back and forth, soooo excited to be at the beach, but she was on the mobile.

Running into the waves, the dog splashed and then ran back to its owner to share the excitement, but she was on the mobile.

She gave a token toss of a ball and the dog was off like a rocket, chasing and enjoying the evening to bring the ball (its own little gift of love) back to the woman, but she was on the mobile.

Has that ever happened to you? Have you ever been like the dog?

Maybe you were speaking to your manager or boss and they were on the phone or simply distracted and not listening. Maybe you were recounting your day to your loved one and they were not listening but simply waiting to tell you about theirs.

It doesn't feel good, does it?

Have you ever been like the woman who is physically there, but not actually present? Maybe your kids were playing but you were just instructing rather than down on the floor on your hands and knees playing FULL ON! Maybe your team were telling you about some of their issues and you listened in a token manner but didn't hear what was truly happening for them. Maybe your partner wanted to engage with you on a fun activity and you were just playing on the surface.

How do you think your kids, your team and your partner felt?

How much better would the dog have felt if the young woman left the phone at home and played FULL ON with the dog? Was really present for the dog? Also, how much better would the woman have felt if she truly connected with the dog and played FULL ON?

If you are going to do something (whether you want to do it or not), I believe you should do it FULL ON. Not just because it is better for others, but also because you will enjoy it more and Get More out of it.

Next time, play with the dog!

**Where do I need to "play with the dog"?**

# Gawk, Talk or Walk?

Do you gawk, talk or walk?

More clearly, do you watch things happen, talk about things you will do or actually make things happen?

There is a time for all three of these, but most people get stuck in the first two. So whether it is in your social life, your business life or even your spiritual life, don't just talk about things or watch things happen, become part of what is happening. Take action. It is more satisfying, more rewarding and more beneficial when you do.

What action will you take today?

**My plan of action:**
_____
_____
_____
_____
_____
_____
_____
_____
_____
_____
_____
_____

# What Would Spiderman Do?

I was speaking to a group last week about Spiderman. Yes, I know – it is not very "businessy", but it is very relevant.

Spiderman's uncle told him "With great power comes great responsibility".

I believe that the opposite also holds true. That is, "With great responsibility comes great power".

Too often I see people dodging responsibility in an organisation.

These same people are also complaining that they "can't change anything".

I implore you to take responsibility, it really isn't that bad. Once you take responsibility for a change you wish to see or a situation you wish to change, you will find that you have power over that situation. You also have power over your own attitude towards that situation.

Where do you need to take responsibility?

**Areas I need to take responsibility:**
_____
_____
_____
_____
_____
_____
_____

# It's the First Day!

This is the first day of the rest of our life.

Why not set up some great habits today that we can continue with each day?

Many will start this day with great vigour; others with fond memories of holidays; and others will be overwhelmed just by looking at their inbox!

How will you start this day? More importantly, how will you end it?

If you can do nothing else, hold a positive attitude that will continue to serve you each day as you work through the day and beyond.

**What habits will I keep today?**
_____
_____
_____
_____
_____
_____
_____
_____
_____
_____
_____
_____
_____
_____

# What is Your Plan?

Don't you hate it when things out of your control have a significant impact on your plans for the day? Whether it is the air conditioner breaking down, staff not arriving on time because of train delays or people being affected by the weather, there are some things you just can't control!

Personally, I love the approach of "Expect the best, but plan for the worst". As soon as I know it is going to be hot, I plan to do detailed work in the morning and easy work in the afternoon. I get that I will be impacted by the heat so I will plan for it. If my air conditioner is strong enough and my energy levels remain high, I will do more detailed work but the plan supports a "worst" outcome.

What about your business and your life? Do you have contingency plans for when things go wrong? Do you know what to do when the unexpected happens?

Life and work become far less stressful when you "Expect the best, but plan for the worst!"

**What is my plan?**

_____
_____
_____
_____
_____
_____
_____
_____

# What Motivates You?

Technically the short answer is "pleasure" and "pain". The truth is we are motivated about the idea of participating in an event or having something (pleasure), or we are motivated by what we think will happen or what we will feel if we DON'T participate in the event or have that thing (pain).

The issue is 80% of people are motivated by pain and only 20% by pleasure – yet pleasure is more sustainable!

Everyone is different. The key is to tap into what motivates us as an individual and use that. So what keeps us going when we want to stop? What drives us when we can't help but move forward?

What is the "idea" or "vision" we can't live without?

Mine is the idea of a business operating how I want it to, a family life that supports me and I can contribute to, and to be the man I can be.

When it comes to business and life, what motivates you?

**What motivates me?**
_____
_____
_____
_____
_____
_____
_____
_____
_____

# How is Your Awareness?

I ride a big motorbike.

It is a great deal of fun but I am the first to admit that it is not without its dangers! Recently, on the way to record a radio play (that's a whole other story) I was nearly run off the road!

To be honest, it happens quite a bit. But there is a secret to surviving it unscathed – maintain your awareness.

I was on a three-lane freeway, behind a big Ford doing 100 km/h (60 m/h) and I knew there was a large white car next to me and a car behind each of us but much further back. All of a sudden, the car next to me indicated and started to change lanes. Nothing gets the adrenaline pumping like a car merging into you! Knowing I had the space, I could brake solidly and drop back letting the driver occupy the space I was previously in without there being any accident. It was then that the driver noticed me and gave me a wave!

Has something like that happened to you? Maybe not on the road, maybe it was at work or with a personal relationship. Something happened that you knew COULD happen but weren't sure if it would.

Again, the secret to minimising the negative impact is to maintain our awareness. If we are too focussed on the details, we miss opportunities or can get blindsided by crisis. Make sure that you keep an awareness of the bigger picture at all times.

What do you need to be aware of today?

# How is Your Copying and Pasting?

I see many people who are masters at copy and paste. But it is not their documents they are copying and pasting, it is themselves!

- They read management books and do exactly what they say.
- They hear jokes and tell them as if they are their own.
- They go on management training and try to be exactly like the training examples.
- They read biographies and try to be like the heroes they idolise.

Lots of copying and pasting.

Don't get me wrong. I am a big fan of training, biographies, books and jokes. But I am a bigger fan of authenticity.

Use the training, the books, the event – whatever it is – as a stimulation to be you. Get the idea, the inspiration, the stimulation and do it your way. Don't be a pale copy of someone or something else. Be a shining example of the authentic you – warts and all!

**How can I be more authentic?**

# Don't Just DO Something – Sit There!

My backyard can have an amazing light and sound show. The sun reflects off the low cloud and changes colours from orange and amber through to pinks, with cloud wisps coloured in different gradients. Meanwhile, the breeze was rustling through the nectarine tree as the neighbour's cat prowled through the yard giving me the "what the hell are you doing sitting on your own back step" look.

I could have taken a photo, but it changes so much and it's not the same. But you may have seen something similar at some other time. It is not the vista that I wanted to share anyway, but the moment.

I had been thinking about things I had on for the week, thinking about a friend who had just ended a relationship, another recovering from surgery, family who had just moved house, how knackered I felt in the heat … you know, a typical day. Taking the time to just step outside and sit there was fabulous.

I took the time to be a human being not a human doing.

Doing this forced me into the moment where I could see that life is okay. Not life and everything will be okay, but it already is okay. Things are great! I have some amazing things happening in my life, I have some amazing people around me (particularly my gorgeous wife!) and some fabulous opportunities. It is fantastically refreshing to be present and sit and appreciate my surroundings.

What about you?

Sometimes you need to remember the age-old truth. Don't just do something, sit there!

# NOTHING CHANGES

Have you noticed how if nothing changes, nothing changes? I know it's a bit obvious, but sometimes it is up to us to change a situation.

For example, I was writing a proposal recently and had been struggling. I just couldn't get into it. So decided a change of geography would shift my mindset. I took my sexy new Netbook to a shopping centre and did the majority of the work in a couple of hours. A simple change got me over my mental block.

What about you? What simple changes can you make when you are stuck – a geographical change (even if it is just changing desks), a physical change (go for a walk) or a mental change (call someone else and ask how they are and don't mention your stuff)?

Next time you get stuck, try something different – you have to make the change happen sometimes.

**What will I change?**
_____
_____
_____
_____
_____
_____
_____
_____
_____
_____

# WHAT INSPIRES YOU?

Inspiration is a critical part of life. It gives us strength, courage, compassion as well as helps us to generate ideas on what to make, what to do, how to behave and who to be in business and in life.

Many people are inspired by truly spectacular athletes who compete. Others, like me, are not. (I really just don't like sport!) We can be inspired in different ways. By nature, by music, by other people, by companies, by children, by art, by theatre, the list goes on.

What is important is to know what kind of things inspire you and then make time to seek out inspiration – not just wait for it to come to you.

So what inspires you?

**What inspires me?**
_____
_____
_____
_____
_____
_____
_____
_____
_____
_____
_____

# Who is Driving?

When it is time to make decisions (important or otherwise), who is driving? Is it you or your ego?

My ego sometimes wants to kick in and I struggle to keep it at bay. When my gorgeous wife and I bought a new car, as a male I wanted the latest and greatest with all the bells and whistles and for it to be brand new and shiny!

Once I was able to put my ego to one side I could see that as much as I wanted a shiny new car, a 10% saving on the cost of the car to have a one-year-old model with 10,000 kilometres on the clock made sense. The difference between the two cars was minimal (16 inch rims vs 17 inch rims).

Even though I could tell myself "I am worth a new car" (and I know I am), the 10% saving was worth it. Now I can invest that 10% rather than just spending it.

When you are making your decisions, how big an impact does your ego have? Don't get me wrong, as the Skyhooks said, "Ego is not a dirty word". But we need to make sure that our ego is not driving us.

So who is driving?

**How does my ego impact me?**
_____
_____
_____
_____
_____
_____

# TAKE IT ALL!

Are you one of these people who wear their annual leave entitlement like a badge of honour?

"I've got 23 weeks of annual leave owing – I haven't had a real holiday in FIVE YEARS!"

Surely you have met people like this in your workplace or know someone like it?

In Australia we get four weeks of annual leave allocated every year – different countries get more than this and others get less. My challenge to you is to make sure you take all of your allocated leave in the year it is allocated. Our bodies and our minds need the time off to relax and renew. This also revives our spirit and sense of wellbeing. So book your leave in now before your colleagues take the good slots available!

Are you up to the challenge?

**When will I take leave?**

# What About Others?

It is very easy to get hung up about how things are for you in a situation, but what about others?

Melbourne was hit by a hailstorm and, unfortunately, my gorgeous wife and I got caught in it in our two-week-old car. The car had serious dents all over it (only the driver's door was spared) and it had to be fixed. While that is disappointing and frustrating for us, what about others?

I saw one guy trying to stop water from flooding down the driveway and into his house. My gorgeous wife's relatives had their patio roof smashed, the TV had images of people with their ceiling caved in, and others got physically injured by hail at an outdoor festival – so we got off very lightly.

Next time you have a situation, stop to think "What about others?"

If you have an irate customer, how would things be from their perspective?

If you have a disagreement with a colleague, what is the impact of the situation on them?

If a friend is not doing or saying what you want, what is going on for them?

Considering the situation from different angles helps you get a better and healthier perspective on your own situation and helps you focus on the solution and not the pain or discomfort of your own situation.

---

**Where do I need to see from another's perspective?**

_____

_____

_____

_____

# What Does Johnny Cash Know?

I was listening to Johnny Cash's American III album which has covers of other songs and the first song is "Won't Back Down" written by Tom Petty. I checked the lyrics and discovered that there are not many.

It is essentially repeating the phrase "I won't back down" and every now and again it's "Well I know what's right, I got just one life in a world that keeps on pushin' me around, but I'll stand my ground ... and I won't back down".

It is the simplicity of the song and the lyrics that amplify its message.

When things get tough do you back down?

Do you stand up for your beliefs?

Do you avoid the difficult conversations, the challenging situations, the draining and demanding actions, the very things that will make you stronger?

Don't back down!

Persistence and commitment will pay off – don't quit before the miracle happens.

Thanks Johnny!

# Is it Too Hard?

We face difficult and challenging situations every day. Whether it is confronting your boss, negotiating a deal, stating an unpopular perspective or making a difficult life choice, we face these situations regularly.

These are tough choices. But you have to ask yourself, is it too hard?

If you choose not to do something because you don't want to, that's fine, but to not do it because it is too hard is the easy way out. It is doing the hard thing that builds our strength. It is facing the challenge that builds our self-esteem regardless of the outcome.

When you are faced with a challenging situation, do you avoid it because you don't want to decide or because it's too hard?

I urge you not to take the easy way out.

**What am I facing that I need to stick with?**

# Is it Good or Bad?

So many things happen in our work and personal lives that we label "good" or "bad". In my experience, it is not what has happened, but how we are feeling that impacts on the label we give it.

There is a psychological term "one up/one down" which usually refers to behaviour in a relationship where one person raises themselves up (in a position of power) by putting the other person down (more of a victim mentality). If we can do it in our relationships with people, we will also do it in our relationships with service providers, businesses, places and circumstances.

My challenge for you is to let go of the good and bad label and adopt the label "interesting" as in, "That's an interesting situation".

It's not good or bad, but interesting.

You can do something with interesting. If it is bad, you are deflated before you start; if it is good then you are okay, but others may be deflated. This also takes into account the old saying, "It's not what happens to you, but how you deal with it that counts".

**What is "interesting" in my life?**
_____
_____
_____
_____
_____
_____
_____

# I'm Not Listening

My gorgeous wife and I went to a family wedding. It was a great time. But families will be families and this family event could not pass without the grapevine passing back some negative message about how I was looking a bit fat!

After years of dieting, exercise (and too much eating) this is THE sensitive area of my life. For some reason, family always knows how to go straight for it. But it's okay, because I'm not listening. When it comes to my health, I will consult my health practitioner rather than take advice from overweight retirees on what I "should" do!

It's the same with the unwanted feedback that I would get from people who worked for the same company I did or were on my team for a short time or came to a meeting once "to give some input". I am more than happy to take advice, recommendation and constructive feedback and I choose from whom I receive it.

Frequently I will ask for it. For me, random feedback from others is like someone else's road rage. I don't know what is going on for them, they don't know what is happening for me, and I don't know them well enough to put any value on their feedback.

So I am not listening!

Who are you listening to?

**Who's opinion do I need to ignore?**
_____
_____
_____
_____

# He Touched Me!

I sing with Mood Swing – you can check out what we sound like at Moodswingchoir.com. We were delighted to be part of the Get Vocal Festival. As well as concerts, there were workshops for artists during the day. A highlight for me was attending the workshop run by the group Tripod.

I had heard so many stories about meeting your heroes and being disappointed. While I may not rank them as "heroes", the Tripod guys are definitely people I admire and look up to. As a speaker, trainer, coach, trade show guru, I am constantly trying to balance the entertainment, education, laughs and valuable resources mix. I had a one-on-one chat with Scott (the one with glasses) who was very humble and gave me some great pointers. He even touched me!

Well ... we shook hands.

It got me thinking, how do we really know how we positively affect people? When we give to them, inspire them, lead them, love them, parent them, coach them, advise them, befriend them or even just talk with them? You never know what impact you will have on those around you simply by sharing what you know and what you have. There are people out there who are better off having been in contact with you. They may even be thinking "(s)he touched me!"

Thanks for being such a cool you. Keep it up.

# What Sort of Impression Do You Make?

There are so many competitors out there. They may not be exactly competitors, but there are companies and businesses that overlap on your patch of the world. It may be a team member "competing" for the next new opportunity, a similar business that competes with yours or someone exhibiting at the same show as you vying for the visitors' attention.

My gorgeous wife reminded me that I make big impressions everywhere I go. Whenever we go shopping, I have fun with the checkout chick (or checkout chap). I figure they are not going anywhere and I know their name (courtesy of the name tag) so I talk to them. They give me the standard "Hi, how are you?" and I make a big impression: "Fantastic. Fabulous. Any happier and I would explode." Maybe not all of those words but some of them! Then have a bit of a laugh with them. When my gorgeous wife went to the supermarket one weekend, the checkout operator said, "Shopping on your own today?" My impression was so big that the checkout operator remembered my gorgeous wife and me and noticed that I wasn't there.

I do the same things when I am working with my exhibitor clients.

I live by the theory, if you are speaking to no one, speak to everyone! When someone walks by the booth I make an impression. I engage with them by simple small talk that can then engage them in a relevant discussion. It could be a memorable one-liner, an engaging question about them, or a statement that makes them laugh. Play with it and see what works.

What about you? What sort of impression do you make? Will they remember you? Will they notice if you are not there? How can you make it bigger, better and more memorable?

# Big Impressions – Part II

It happened again!

I am not sure if I should be surprised or not that the very next day after I wrote on making a big impression, it happened again.

My gorgeous wife and I are big fans of the Coco Lounge in Glen Waverley. In particular we like to go there for a Fraus. For the uninitiated, this is a thick European hot chocolate. Typically, I like it extra thick so it becomes like chocolate custard. Yes, yes, I know I am a bit of a foody.

Anyway, after seeing a movie we adjourned to Coco Lounge for the Fraus. When we asked for one, the waiter indicated that they no longer served them. Naturally I went "Noooooooo!!" rather loudly. We had a few laughs and then a coffee instead. As we paid, I was speaking to the manager and discussing why they stopped selling the Fraus and he basically said that they were not selling enough and the product would be wasted. I joked about how would I live without it and then he said "Wait a second".

He brought back to me 1 KILO of Fraus mix. He gave it to me free of charge. It was a very generous gesture and makes me love Coco Lounge even more! But it wouldn't have happened if I didn't make a significant impression. Let's face it, my good looks didn't make it happen!

So what will happen if you make a big impression? Try it and see!

**How will I make a big impression?**
_____
_____
_____
_____
_____

# Need More Adventure?

When was your last "adventure"? I don't mean tracking wombats through the state forest (although some people may have done that). I mean done something that is an adventure for you. Something that gets your heart racing, your adrenalin flowing and your sense of anticipation at full alert.

So many people get into the rut of everyday life. All of a sudden it becomes: get up, go to work, come home, have dinner, watch TV, go to bed and repeat. Even if you have a few hobbies like sport, study or theatre thrown in, it can get repetitive. So where's the adventure?

Your routine may be different. It may include flying around the countryside exhibiting at expos and trade shows, but we have all had that feeling where one show just blends into another. Sometimes we need a bit of adventure to break the routine. (By the way, the adventure can frequently give us ideas to use at the next show!)

My challenge to you is to plan for and then have some adventure in your life. Plan and do something within two months' time, something that challenges and excites you and that you are interested in doing.

It could be:

- Ten minutes of stand-up at an open mic night
- Karaoke singing with friends
- Auditioning for a local theatre production
- Booking guitar lessons
- Going skiing
- Writing a book

What is your adventure?

**What adventures will I take?**

# What Could You Do?

My gorgeous wife loves Mustangs. A few years ago we spent four days bringing one back from Queensland. Her name was Candy, a 1965 Mustang Coupe.

Unfortunately, due to a miscalculation and an "interesting" fuel gauge, we ran out of fuel on the Hume! I got the job of walking back to the servo while my gorgeous wife stayed with Candy. After 15 minutes of walking a car pulled over and the guy said, "My wife is with your wife and the 20 litres of petrol I had in the boot". It was a fabulous thing to hear!

About 100 vehicles had driven past. Our car was obviously not going anywhere, my gorgeous wife was resting on the boot waiting, so why did he stop when no one else did? He was the only one to ask himself the question "What can I do?" Everyone else could see we needed help but they took no action.

What about you? What signs or signals have you seen that you KNOW you need to act on but haven't? Team members that need help, family members that need assistance, sales figures not being met, strangers that want the newspaper you have just finished with, projects that need attention – you KNOW what they need.

Take the action and reap the reward!

**What signs do I need to act on?**
_____
_____
_____
_____

# Should I be Committed?

For many years, people have said that I am crazy. As I found watching Alice in Wonderland recently, all the best people are! They say that I should be committed, but what they don't understand is that I already am. Let me explain.

I love the saying, "In for a penny, in for a pound". Quite simply, if you are going to do something, give it all you have. So when a client said that the theme of their gala ball was Australian and New Zealand icons, I couldn't just dress as the icon, I had to BE the icon. I chose Dame Edna Everage.

The reality is it wasn't pretty. A 190 cm tall, hairy bloke squeezed into a pink sequin and feather dress just isn't right! I had trouble with the shoes so I made my own with aluminium foil; not pretty, but effective! They thought I was insane, but I wasn't, I was just committed to what the client wanted. The client absolutely loved it! None of their team will forget the event in a hurry, for a whole lot of reasons, one of which was the MC!

What about you? Are you committed to what you want to achieve? Do you focus on your goals and targets on a daily basis? Are you working towards getting your goals and not just setting them? Do you throw yourself at life with abandon or just stick a toe in the water?

Life is to be lived. I believe you need to squeeze the very last drop out of every day because it is not coming back again. Maybe I am crazy. I am definitely committed and I wouldn't have it any other way.

How committed are you?

# NEED A CHALLENGE?

Some of you may know that I am a "nutritional overachiever" (code for carries too much body fat). What makes it worse is that I am not a fan of sport or exercise. I know my lifestyle is very sedentary, but I just couldn't face a gym full of lycra-covered beautiful people (and that's just the guys!). A friend of mine, Super Steph, suggested I do Step Into Life, which is group personal training outdoors.

So for the past 16 months I have been running around like an idiot at really early hours of the day because it is in the best interests of my body. Apparently some endorphins will kick in soon and make me feel fantastic, but I am still waiting! As part of this foolishness (which also lets me talk for an hour and tell stupid jokes because I know the others are not going anywhere so I have a trapped audience) they have a "winter challenge".

For six weeks we had to do extra activities. As much as I didn't want to, I had to. I know my body needs it and I was part of the legendary Team 4 and I didn't want to let them down.

The challenges were:

- Do an additional 30 minutes of exercise every day (and that is not jumping to conclusions!).
- Be in bed by 10.00 pm.
- Drink two litres of water a day (this is tough so I use soda water – bubbles! Yay!).
- Do daily push-ups, starting at ten and adding five every day.
- Turn up to the sessions I said I would.

How can you challenge yourself to get to your goals that little bit quicker? It may hurt a little but you will forget the pain when you achieve your goal that little bit sooner.

# Do You Hear Voices?

I like the old saying "The person who says something can't be done is usually interrupted by someone doing it". I am not sure if it is a quote, saying, proverb or adage, but its meaning is true.

It may surprise you who the person is saying that it can't be done: it's you!

I suspect you will be telling other people they can achieve their dreams, but you may hold yourself back. Have you ever heard that little voice saying:

"Who are you to attempt this?"
"There is no way you can do it."
"What if it doesn't work?"
"Don't bite off more than you can chew."
"Think of all the things you will have to do and you are not that lucky."

I know these voices because I have heard them a lot over the years.

I was reminded of a fantasy I had years ago where I would be paid a lot of money to sing or play music. It popped into my head as I was returning from singing at a sell-out gig with my vocal group Mood Swing. At the same gig where we were paid well and sold CDs as well.

What do you think is impossible for you? What do you stop yourself from doing before you even get started?

It's time to change the voice in your head.

**Where do I stop myself?**
_____
_____
_____

GET MORE INSPIRATION | 65

# Is it Fantasy or Planning?

I bought some tickets in the Royal Melbourne Hospital Home Lottery. It is not something I have done before. Like many people, I will buy a $2 or $5 raffle ticket here or there, but it is rare to spend $100 or more on a ticket. I just figured I have one chance in 26 of winning a prize and one chance in 80,000 of winning the grand prize. Those are far better odds than Tattslotto (one chance in over 8 million) and the money goes to a good cause.

Discussing the prizes with my gorgeous wife, we started planning what we would do when we won the Aston Martin Vantage (she likes Aston Martins). Which of the other cars would we sell, where would we park it, where would we drive it and that kind of thing. It struck me, is it fantasy or is it good planning?

It's a bit of both really. In the same way when you are planning a new business venture, you need to consider some of the finer points and put yourself in the position of achieving what you want. It gets the mind ready for it and you will already know how to deal with the situation happening. Yes, it is a bit of fantasy, but it is planning for what your hard work will bring about.

Where do you need to do some more of this kind of planning?

**When will I do some daydreaming?**

# Do You Look After Yourself?

I was suffering from "man flu". Men are always the last to know that they have it. Luckily my gorgeous wife was able to point it out to me. It is when a man has a slight cold but they think it is the end of the world!

Now, I am not a believer in "soldiering on". I believe that when my body is ill I need to rest and let it get better. Consequently, I cancelled several business and social appointments. Now, I could have gone along but it was just not worth it. There was a slight chance I could have infected the person I was meeting (and depending on their air-conditioning system, half of the people on their floor too!), I would have been foggy-headed and not had my wits about me for the meeting and, most importantly, my body would be straining to soldier on and not simply recover.

So I stayed home, taking my hippy pills (horseradish, garlic and vitamin C) and let my body rest. Three days later and I was feeling fabulous. Compare that to many who soldier on and "just can't seem to shake it".

When you get ill, do you look after yourself? Not just when you have a cold (or man flu), but also when you are grieving, distressed, or just need a doona day. I am not saying we should all have a sick day. What I am saying is you HAVE to look after yourself and do what it takes to maintain a healthy body, mind and spirit.

How well do you look after yourself?

# Why Would You Tear Them Down?

We had 18 trees cut down in our front and back yard. It was not something we did lightly and it does prompt the question, "Why would you tear them down?"

The majority of them were pine trees planted as a hedge over 20 years ago. It was a great idea. It gave extra privacy from the neighbours and passers-by as well as some wind protection. For the first couple of years they did their job well, but over time things changed. The owners of the house got new tenants in who didn't prune the trees, as they needed. The larger trees dropped more needles. The ground beneath the trees stopped growing lawn as it was starved of nutrients and sunlight. The path under the trees was not maintained and became overgrown with weeds, and the trees grew so tall that they blocked nearly all the light from the northern sun.

With minimal light, moss started growing on the roof and on the path up to the front door making it slippery and unsafe in the wet. What started as a great idea grew way out of control.

Have you ever seen this happen in the workplace? A system, process, work idea, project, guiding principle or cultural element of an organisation starts off well, has great intent and then becomes the nightmare of the business. I have seen it many times.

Sometimes a "mild trim" is not enough, you have to rip it out at the roots and start again!

So my gorgeous wife and I are now planning the redesign of the gardens including replanting more suitable and more productive trees.

What about you? What behemoths need to be torn down so fresh new ideas and practices can flourish?

# Would You Like a Drink?

One of the things that many people forget to do is drink. I don't mean whip down to the pub and have a sly bevy, I mean drink plenty of fluids during the day. Too often we can get so involved in what we are working on that we neglect to have enough fluids.

This leads to the typical symptoms of being thirsty: dry lips and also headaches, dizziness and cramping.

So the question is how much fluid should you have?

The correct answer is, "it depends". The old standard of eight cups (two litres) of water a day is not entirely accurate. There are many factors to consider. The best thing to do is review the simple guide on the Kidney Health Australia website. There is some great information there.

Personally, I swear by the old backpacker trick I learned while travelling (it gets handed down from generation to generation). If your urine is yellow, you are dehydrated so you need to drink more fluids. Water is the best fluid but others will contribute to re-hydrating you.

So to keep your head clear, your mind focussed, your day on track (and your urine clear), drink more fluids!

Can I offer you a drink?

**How can I support myself to drink more fluids?**
_____
_____
_____
_____

# Are You Harry?

As a self-confessed geek, I looked forward to the final two Harry Potter films. I had read the books so I knew what was going to happen and I still looked forward to them! The people who least looked forward to them would be the three actors in the lead roles: Daniel Radcliffe, Rupert Grint and Emma Watson.

The reason they would not be looking forward to the end of the Harry Potter films is not the end of the money. According to trash magazines they will have earned enough cash from the films to last them a couple of lifetimes. It is not the end of the fame because they will always be Harry, Ron and Hermione (in fact many may remember their character name but not their real one). The reason they are not looking forward to it is that it is likely to be the end of their acting career.

They will always be Harry, Ron and Hermione. Even in a different film, people will say "It's got Harry Potter in it". Even though they have all done some other work to try and increase their reputation, they will struggle to get past their larger-than-life characters. Many movie projects will not want that baggage.

So are you Harry?

Have you done what you do for so long that it is the only thing people (including your boss) know you for?

Does the baggage of "Oh, they are the one who does …" follow you around? Or have you tried on a few other roles?

Have you expanded your skillset to learn new and relevant skills?

Have you volunteered for different projects within the business to show you can do other things?

Have you done interesting things outside of the workplace to build a rounded character? Have you shown yourself you can do many amazing things?

Don't just be Harry. Be as many people or roles as you can.

**What new roles do I need to embrace?**

# What were You Thinking?

Mum was down from Queensland visiting and she was spending a couple of days with me. As well as going for a spin in Candy (the V8 Mustang that is my gorgeous wife's car), we chatted and did a few things. I made my famous Frangelico and walnut brownies (let me know if you want the recipe). This is when the strange thing happened. Just after I poured the mix into the bowl, I turned to Mum and asked "Do you want to lick the spoon?"

It was like a science fiction movie. All of a sudden I was swept back to when I was a kid and Mum would ask me, "Do you want to lick the spoon?" It was so not how the situation was "supposed" to be. But the more I thought about it, the more I realised that it is EXACTLY how life is supposed to be.

Each generation matures to take over the role of the previous one. It happens all around us. So why do we fight it?

It is because of what we are thinking. We hold ourselves back with old ways of thinking. We have ideas of what our parents should do, our boss should do, our colleagues should do, what we can't do, what subordinates shouldn't do … the ideas and rules of what we can and can't do continue on!

Change your thinking!

You can parent your parents, you can boss your boss, you can lead your leaders, and you can do all the things you tell yourself you can't. It is okay to say no to your boss. You can submit your ideas to the discussion even if you are a junior and haven't been there long.

Change your thinking and you will change your life.

Go get 'em!

# WHAT ABOUT ME?

Something funny happened.

Like most people, my gorgeous wife and I use shampoo. We bought some new shampoo and started using it. A couple of days later, my gorgeous wife asked, "What do you think of the new shampoo?"

Personally, I don't use a great deal of shampoo. It probably has something to do with the fact that I am balding (but I am still in denial about it). So I mentioned this to my gorgeous wife and also that I was not that fussed about it.

Her response, "I meant, what do you think about the new shampoo in my hair!"

Ooops!!

I should have realised that. She does have resplendent hair that cascades halfway down her back (mine is just back hair). But I was too focussed on myself. I wasn't considering the intent of her comment. Based on the number of conversations we have never had about my hair versus the ones we have had about hers, I should have known it was not about me.

What about you?

When you communicate, are you more concerned about yourself or those with whom you are communicating?

Do you listen to what the other person is saying, and trying to say, or is your focus on what you want to say?

Is your focus on the conversation, or on reaching the mutually sought outcome?

# Have You Got What You Need?

I spent six hours with a Dingo. I don't mean the protected native dog of Australia; I mean the piece of earthmoving equipment.

You see, my gorgeous wife and I are a typical couple in the suburbs. Some weekends we like to dig in the garden and some weekends we like to knock down the side wall, dig out six cubic metres of earth, create a massive new vegie garden and then replace the earth with road base so we can park one of our many vehicles up the side of the garage, then we like to spread the nine cubic metres of topsoil on the new lawn area where the old pine trees were cut down.

Now I don't know about you, but shifting a total of 21 cubic metres of earth by hand is a huge effort. Let alone digging out that dirt at the side of the shed that was full of tree roots. So I decided to make it easier for myself and get the right gear. So I spent six hours with a Dingo. It made the job a whole lot easier and quicker. It was a whole lot of fun too!

I have found time and time again that having what I need makes a massive difference. Accounting software does a better job than a spreadsheet; waterproof ski gear is better than jeans; sunglasses are better than squinting … you see the theme.

Have you got what you need?

If there is something you need to do at work or at home, get the right gear. It makes the job easier, quicker and more rewarding.

**What gear do I need?**

# Have You Told Anyone?

I caught up with a friend and he told me a strange story.

My friend (let's call him Simon, because that is his name) works for a multinational with an Asia Pacific regional office in Singapore.

His direct boss is based in this office. Now Simon doesn't see his boss much, but it is an IT company so they stay in touch with emails and video conferencing and the like.

He was at an internal meeting with another colleague from Singapore. Simon participated as usual and they were able to come up with a resolution to a particular issue. His colleague went back to Singapore and Simon thought nothing of it.

The next day, Simon received a text from his boss saying something along the lines of, "I have just heard about the great job you guys did. Thank you for your contribution. I understand it made a difference and I wanted to let you know I appreciate it."

Wow!

It had a significant impact on Simon. It confirmed for him that he has a great boss, works at a great company and he is truly valued.

Before you start thinking "My boss never says anything like that", put the shoe on the other foot. Who have you said something like that to?

Have you told anyone that you appreciate their work lately?

Research has shown that genuine compliments have a more positive impact than a pay rise. So who needs one? Your boss, your team members, your cleaner, your security guard, the receptionist, the person in the café, your partner, your kids, your friends or your family? I am sure there is someone.

So have you told anyone lately?

**Who do I need to compliment?**

# Are They Eating out of Your Hand?

My gorgeous wife and I regularly get away. One trip was to Wye River. It is a stunning location where mountains meet the sea. The glorious gum trees are filled with bird life. We have seen cockatoos, rosellas, willy wagtails (ornithologists will know them as *Rhipidura leucophrys*!), currawongs and king parrots.

I decided I wanted to get up close and I finally had them eating out of my hand. You can use the same process to get your customers eating out of your hand.

1. Go where your customer is – I went on to the balcony when the birds were there.
2. Give them what they want – I had broken bits of biscuit that I knew they liked.
3. Make it easy for them – I put some crumbs on the railing and then held my open handful of crumbs next to it.
4. Support them and make them comfortable – I held my hand steady and gave them more crumbs as they stood on my hand.
5. Show gratitude – As they fed I was saying thank you for visiting us.
6. Celebrate your success – The rest of us staying at the house came out to say hello to the king parrots.

What about you? Do you have your customers eating out of your hands? Use this process and you soon can!

---

**How can I apply this process?**

_____

_____

# Have You Got Your Fat Bob?

Before you get too excited, let me tell you that a Fat Bob is a type of Harley Davidson motorcycle.

Maybe your desire is not for a Fat Bob, maybe it's a BMW or a piece of jewellery or an overseas holiday. How are you going with your dream?

A client and friend of mine, Paul, has always wanted a brand new Harley. But the story is not as simple as: set goal, worked hard and got goal.

Paul wanted a brand new Harley, but along the way settled for second-hand ones. In fact, he had 23 of them before he got his brand new Fat Bob!

But still, it's not that simple. On his way to work, a kangaroo decided to try and knock him off his bike. This resulted in major leg and back damage, several operations and coming up with an ingenious way to store crutches on the bike as he rode!

And still, it is not that simple. He said to me, "Mate, my journey is far from over. At least two, probably four operations are scheduled during the year with a whole lot of recovery work".

THAT is what this is about. Realising that the journey is not over until they lay you in the coffin. There will always be hiccups and barriers along the way. There will always be more to do. There will always be reasons to give up. Keep the focus on what you desire and keep working towards it, one step at a time. Get the support you need and live life, enjoying today. Who knows what tomorrow brings?!

For some, tomorrow brings a Fat Bob. What will your tomorrow bring?

# Are You Sure it's Not Funny?

Life is pretty serious. I mean, just look at the people on public transport, people walking down the street, strolling through the supermarket, huddled around the stock market numbers, watching over kiddies, driving cars ... How serious is everyone!

I don't get it.

People seem to have so much more fun when they laugh, or even just smile. Wouldn't you think they would want to do it more? Wouldn't you think that every situation has to have at least some fun part to it, some element that could at least bring on a smile? Even a boring situation like a boardroom meeting?

Here's what I did. I focussed on having a smile as my default expression. Not an easy thing to do but with practice it works. So when I walk down the street, go on a train, ride my motorbike, talk with strangers, I smile. It makes me feel good and others join in.

Want to join me too? Today, put a smile on your dial.

I DARE YOU!!

**Where do I need to smile?**
_____
_____
_____
_____
_____

# Do You Lead or Will You Get out of the Way?

Here is a micro-course in leadership.

Some of you may think you do not have a leadership position. Well, you would be wrong! You are the leader of your own life.

So even if you work on your own, these points can help you in getting what you want out of life, personally and professionally. To make it easier to digest I have broken it into three principles. Each principle focuses you on three things.

Thinking about these items is not enough. You need to put these three principles into action.

## Part 1: Your three skills are:

**Focus** – Where is your focus? What you focus on will get achieved. So have some kind of reminder (a picture, statement or symbol) to help you and your team focus on what is really IMPORTANT and not just urgent.

**Measure** – What gets measured gets improved. How will you measure your improvement or progress? Is it numeric, do you need surveys, should you involve your customers?

**Delegate** – Get More done by doing less. It is too easy to say "But I can do it quicker". Work with your team to train them up to do what needs to be done. The effort will bring great returns.

How will you implement these three principles?

## Part 2: Are you a leader?

I was at band camp improving my music skills (I play a bass guitar). I was working on my communication and leadership skills. Even when jamming, a direction is needed, support of the others is invaluable, and as a bass player sometimes all I do is play a boring two notes over and over (and over and over ...) but this lays the foundation for others to build on.

Your work is probably the same. Your three leadership skills in Part 2 are:

**Own it** – With great responsibility comes great power. Taking ownership of a situation gives you the power to improve it or get out of it. Sitting around acting helpless keeps you in it.

**Listen** – We have two ears and one mouth so use them in that ratio. So often we are busy telling others what we think that we miss out on their valuable input. We also leave them feeling unheard and demotivated.

**Decide** – Make decisions. Even the wrong decision is better than no decision. A decision leads to movement and action. This will lead to a result. If it is not the right result, change your decision.

## Part 3: Plus a bonus!

The last part of our leadership micro-course includes a bonus.

This time there are FOUR skills to focus on. Your four leadership skills are:

**Act** – Talking and thinking won't get the results that action will. Leadership is not a theory, it is an action. So take action and be the leader you want to be.

**Authenticity** – Be yourself. Get inspiration and ideas from others but be yourself. Adapt the ideas and skills to your style. It will then be natural for you to lead.

**Appreciate** – Thank the people who support you and your team, regardless of how small their contribution. Words and gestures of appreciation make a far bigger difference than you can imagine. Even if someone is doing what they are supposed to, showing appreciation makes a big difference.

**Share** – A leader takes a little more than their fair share of the blame and a little less than their fair share of the accolades. Have some humility. It will make you more attractive as a leader and will create a massive sense of loyalty in those around you.

Don't forget to measure your progress. Using these ten simple leadership skills will make a huge difference in what you can achieve as a team in your personal and professional life.

Go for it!

### How will I apply these principles?

_____
_____
_____
_____
_____
_____
_____
_____
_____
_____
_____
_____
_____
_____
_____

# How Come I am Not Perfect?

I have been spending a bit of time playing the bass lately.

There is a part of me that wants to pick it up and be an absolute guru at it straight away! The reality is that it is not going to happen. I need to put in the effort.

When I left university and started my IT career, I wanted to be the CEO straightaway. When I started singing I wanted to be a star straightaway. How come I am not perfect at anything straightaway?

I recall when Goanna won the Best New Artist award back in the 1980s, the lead singer commented that it took them ten years to be an overnight success. I am certain Susan Boyle's overnight success was preceded by years of practice, training and commitment. In Malcolm Gladwell's book *Outliers* he says that the magic number is 10,000 hours of practice to be a leader in a field.

The secret to these 10,000 hours is actually just doing them and doing them one hour at a time.

In the area you want to be a guru – work, home, guitar or even bass guitar – just keep doing it one hour at a time as best as you can. This is the shortcut to success!

**Where do I need to spend 10,000 hours?**
_____
_____
_____
_____

# WHAT IS THE REALITY?

Someone, somewhere has really upset Mother Nature. Friends in the US and Europe are telling me about massive snow dumps and incredible low temperatures. Here in Australia we have flooding, cyclones, bushfires and unseasonal rainfall. Can whoever upset Mother Nature please apologise!

With all the rain in Melbourne, we were also affected. One broken tile in our roof led to a massive hole in the ceiling of our lounge room where the plaster used to be. It is amazing what one broken tile can do.

As I was bemoaning this situation to my gorgeous wife, I had a flash of reality. There were people in flood-ravaged Brisbane or cyclone-ravaged Queensland who would be happy to have just a broken tile on their house.

The reality is that while I had a problem it was really rather insignificant compared to the problems of others.

The same can be said for problems we find in our working lives. At the time they can seem insurmountable, inconvenient and a massive block to achieving your goal. Looking at your situation with a healthy perspective does a lot to remove the emotional blockages. You can then focus on addressing the issue one step at a time.

So, when you next have an insurmountable issue, what is the reality?

**What problem am I over-exaggerating?**
_____
_____
_____
_____

# But Who are You Really?

I love weekends when I am surrounded by kids. One weekend consisted of:

- Friday night with my brother's three kids where we had an impromptu disco, karaoke and singer impersonation session.
- Sunday afternoon my gorgeous wife's brother's three kids dropped over as I was harvesting the sunflowers, and in their excitement nearly slammed the car door on one another.
- Sunday night at a friend's place where their two kids were doing what kids do: sleeping on the dog, planning time to spend with dad for the week, diving on the couch, showing off their chooks and vegie garden.

I LOVE the enthusiasm and vibrancy of kids. They represent true authenticity. Who they are right now is who they are. They happily tell you how they feel, they have opinions on most things, their emotions show easily and quickly, and you pretty much know how they feel and who they are. The same cannot be said for many adults.

All my life I have been accused of being "childish". So many people have told me to grow up. A friend who works in child psychiatry said she would assess me at being about 14 years old. Legendary baseballer Chili Davis is attributed as having said "Growing old is mandatory; growing up is optional". I believe we can be mature, professional and sophisticated combined with childlike enthusiasm and energy.

So who are you REALLY? Are you really how you behave or have years of "shoulds" changed how you are in the world? Does your inner child need to burst out and say hello?

Who are you REALLY?

**Who am I and where does my inner child need to come out?**

# Have You Got the Right Gear?

When I first learnt to snow ski, I borrowed the ski gear from friends and rented the essentials. My first couple of times were not pleasant experiences. My feet hurt in the boots, there was a hole in the ski pants so I was wet and cold to the bone and the trusty rental skis had a mind of their own!

After a while I bought my own ski outfit. I was then toasty warm but with sore feet and a misguided sense of direction. I finally got sick of sore ankles and bought some boots that actually fit properly and some parabolic skis that did all the hard work for me.

Skiing was now a completely different experience. I was warm, skiing was effortless, I could go anywhere, I had faith in my equipment and most importantly, I really enjoyed the day.

The right gear makes all the difference.

It's the same with your work. Have you got the right gear? For years I had been "putting up" with a second-hand computer I was given. My audio and video processing took ages, but it was what I had. When I took delivery of what I call MEGA PC – loads of memory (12 GB), huge hard drive with auto backup, fast access ports and large monitors – my first reaction was "Why didn't I do this ages ago?" Granted, the technology prices keep coming down, but I forgot the important concept that the right gear makes all the difference. It is worth the investment of time, effort and money to get it.

Have you got the right gear to do what you need to?

# WHAT DO YOU WANT?

It has often been said that you will get what you want once you want what you've got.

The book *Affluenza* by Clive Hamilton talks about how many people spend money they don't have buying things they don't need to impress people they don't like.

Whether it is the "stuff" or people you have in life, or the clients and customers you have, once you start showing appreciation for them, you can't help but attract more of the clients, customers, "stuff" and people into your life. You just have to show your existing ones how much you appreciate them.

What do you want and what have you already got?

**What do I really want?**
_____
_____
_____
_____

**What have I already got?**
_____
_____
_____
_____

# Who are You Selling to?

So many salespeople run around trying to get new clients, they forget about their existing ones. One company I was working with is in severe financial crisis. They were so focussed on getting new customers to get them out of debt that they forgot about their existing ones.

It is a commonly accepted figure that it is five times easier to sell to existing customers than to get a new one. Soooo many people know this, but most RARELY act on it. So today, what additional or repeat product or service can you sell to your existing client base?

Who are you selling to?

---

**What do I need to tell my existing customers that I can do for them?**

_____
_____
_____
_____
_____
_____
_____
_____
_____
_____
_____
_____
_____
_____

# WHAT INSPIRES YOU?

They say life is short. Billy Connolly pointed out it is the longest thing you ever do!

For many people, one week is the same as the next … is the same as the next … is the same as the next.

What inspires you to get up each day and get on with your life?

Is it your pay cheque? The idea of living a better life? Is it contribution to others? Is it providing for your loved ones?

If you don't have inspiration, how can you expect to face the day energised and ready to rock?

**What inspires me?**

# Are You Crazy?

My gorgeous wife and I had a great week in Bali. On the last day, we had time to fill in between checkout and our midnight flight. So we went for massages, manicures and pedicures. As they were pedicuring my toes I asked, "Can I have purple toenails?"

The young girls just laughed at me. Then they realised I was genuine. So we went through the colours until I got the purple I was after.

As she was painting she jokingly asked, "Do you want a flower?" Naturally I said, "Yes please!"

Again she laughed but did it.

Their reaction was one of "Are you crazy?"

Many times I have done things and normal, sane, professional people have asked "Are you crazy?"

Sure, I could have done the normal thing and not had my toenails painted. But I would never have seen an artist at work creating flowers with nail polish.

Sure, I could have stayed in Melbourne and not taken a job in Wahgunyah three hours from Melbourne, but I would never have had the exposure to the managing director of the company I was working for when I was one of ten people there rather than one of 200 in Melbourne.

Sure, I could have not competed in Raw (the stand-up comedy competition), but I would not have been able to get the experience in honing my funny bone or know how to hit other people's.

My biggest fear is that my life will be "beige". Being crazy or doing crazy things gives me experiences that most don't have, understanding many search for, perspective few ever see and joy many seek. So when people ask me "Are you crazy?" I reply, "Yes, and thanks for the compliment".

What about you?

Are you crazy?

Try it; it does wonders for you.

**How can I be more crazy?**

# WHY DO YOU DO IT?

What better way to start the day than staying in bed reading a book. One of my favourite authors is Stephen King. Not because I am a horror fan (far from it); I just love the way he writes.

His short stories are some of my favourites. Many don't realise he wrote (among others) *The Green Mile*, *The Mist*, *Running Man*, *Stand By Me* and *Hearts in Atlantis*.

In the introduction to *Just After Sunset*, he mentions that he writes not for the money, not for the fame and not for himself. He writes for those who will read his stories. He writes to create a better experience for them. He is also serious about his writing. In his non-fiction book *On Writing*, he says if you are serious about writing you need to read four hours a day and write four hours a day.

So why do you do what you do? Is it for the money, to provide for those you love, to master the art of it, is it a game or is it to improve the lives of your end customer? How much effort do you spend at your skill?

**Why do I do what I do?**
_____
_____
_____
_____
_____
_____
_____
_____

# How Do You Deal With it?

On a holiday to Bali, I came face to face with nature. It was an interesting and unexpected encounter.

It is not often you have a monkey on your back! The guide had mentioned that if a monkey did interact with us to remain calm. I did get a bit of a fright. I had no idea what it was going to do. I didn't know how the situation would end, I didn't know what the monkey wanted and I certainly was not prepared for the second monkey (who seemed to want to take my shirt off!).

Life is a bit like that too. Things happen without prior warning and you have to deal with them as best and as quickly as you can.

You can find yourself in a situation you didn't plan on and like with the monkey, you need to remain calm and deal with it.

So how do you deal with these situations?

Watch the video of the monkey on my back at http://bit.ly/WarwicksMonkey

**How do I deal with unexpected problems?**
_____
_____
_____
_____
_____
_____

# Are You Used to It?

I had to go to Portland, Oregon, for work. I took a drive out to the Colorado River Gorge. I call it drive-by tourism. I took some photos as I drove. It was astounding to have Mt Hood looming so close. I was blown away to be driving around and have this amazing snow-capped mountain in the background.

I guarantee you that many locals will not even see it. We get used to things and don't notice how special they are. It is not taking it for granted, because I am sure the locals love it, it is just that you see it so often you get used to it and it blends into the background.

Are some of your customers, your team members, your support staff, or your family the same? I am sure you know how special they are, how much they mean to you, but it is easy to get used to having them around and having them do things for you.

So are you used to it? Make sure they know how much they mean to you and your business.

**What do I take for granted?**
_____
_____
_____
_____
_____
_____
_____
_____

# Smile!

A new friend who attended one of my presentations liked what I had to say about smiling. She found a poem that someone had given her and shared it with me. I love it! So I wanted to share it with you.

## Smile For You

Smiling is infectious; you catch it like the flu
When someone smiled at me today, I started smiling too.
I passed around the corner and someone saw my grin,
When he smiled I realised I'd pass it onto him.
I thought about that smile and then I realised its worth,
A single smile, just like mine, could travel round the earth.
So if you feel a smile begin, don't leave it undetected,
Let's start an epidemic quick and get the world infected!

Now you can pop a smile on your face and pass it on!

**Where do I need to smile more?**

# Can You Do it Again?

According to an American Express Global Customer Service Barometer Survey, 25% of Australians think businesses take their custom for granted while 10% think businesses don't care about them at all! Is your business like that? Is the service you give like that?

Speaking to the master of Million Dollar Relationships, Danielle Storey, the secret to continuous excellence in customer service is consistency. While it is important to have some kind of process to provide excellent customer service, once is not enough. Whether you are giving great service to your customers, your internal customers or even your suppliers, you need to be able to do it time and time and time again.

From simply answering the phone in a professional manner, welcoming people who come into your business, thanking customers for paying their invoices, or having an ongoing loyalty program, it is consistency that really counts. Make sure your systems and processes are simple and straightforward enough so you can do it again and again and again.

**What customer service processes do I need?**

# Is it Really You?

Who are you? No I mean REALLY?

Too often we have masks we wear at work and then a different one for friends and then another for family and then another for our charity groups. After putting so many different masks on we often lose who we really are.

On top of that we have the expectations from society, our parents, our partners, our colleagues, our superiors, our inferiors and even ourselves.

So who are you really? What do you stand for? What do you like? What don't you like? There are so many things that go into making up who you really are. Once you know, BE the authentic you.

You don't need to be a certain way because others expect it or want it or need it. Be the authentic YOU. That way no one will ever need to ask:

Is it really you?

**How can I be more "me"?**

# Is it OK to Give Compliments?

I love looking at ladies' shoes – particularly Nine West. Not in a fetish kind of way, just in an "I appreciate them" kind of way. Guys' shoes always seem so boring, but ladies' shoes have so many fabulous styles.

Over the years I have commented to women when I like their shoes. Most often they are complete strangers to me. I figure they have put a lot of effort and money into looking good and if I like their shoes, they would want to know.

However, I was informed that giving compliments was "not nice"!

My gorgeous wife and I were having lunch at a winery on the Mornington Peninsula in Victoria. As we were chatting, a couple walked past on the outside of the café. My gorgeous wife pointed out to me the woman's boots – they were really cool. We then continued with our lunch.

As we were leaving, I pushed my chair back and bumped into the diner behind me. It happened to be that woman with the boots. I apologised for bumping into her and then said, "By the way, they are really nice shoes you are wearing. Are they uncomfortable?"

"No they really aren't even though you think they would be", she replied.

I then went to pay the bill.

As I was waiting for the credit card to process, someone tapped me on the shoulder. It was the shoe woman's boyfriend. He got my attention and then said, "You have just paid my girlfriend a beautiful compliment. Don't do it again, it is not very nice."

I said "Okay" and he went on his way.

I must confess it spun me out a little. Why would someone not want to receive a compliment? Why should someone care that a random stranger said something nice about a piece of clothing their partner was wearing? Was it wrong of me to compliment the shoe woman?

I will continue to give strangers compliments. I think that one guy was a bit possessive. If I was shoe woman, I would be considering whether I wanted to spend a lot of time with someone who goes out of his way to discourage compliments!

Compliments are free and they are also priceless. They go straight to the warm and squidgy bit inside you that jumps with delight when you receive one. For some reason, compliments from strangers make that jump even bigger. It is more than okay to give compliments. It is one of the best things you can do.

So thanks for reading this, and by the way … I like your shoes!

**Who do I need to give a compliment to?**

# WHAT ABOUT ME?

It happens to all of us. We have days when our energy is down, our emotions are down and even our mood is down. Everything seems too hard and you just want to get back into bed and tell the world to go away.

When clients ask me what is the best thing to do when you get in these spots or have periods of depression, I tell them to do this.

- Get up
- Have a shower
- Put on some nice clothes
- Leave the house
- Go to a friend's place
- Ask what is happening in their life and DO NOT talk about yourself

Thinking about ourselves and asking "What about me?" does nothing to lift a depressed state – frequently it makes it worse. So put yourself to one side and focus on somebody else and what is happening for them. Once you get out of your own way and stop asking "What about me?", you will be amazed how your mood, energy and emotions shift.

**What will I do when I next feel down?**
_____
_____
_____
_____
_____
_____

# What are You Doing?

In business there is always so much to do.

You are getting the sale, servicing the sale, supporting the sale or looking for the next sale. It seems the bigger your business grows, the more peripheral work needs to be done. By "peripheral work" I mean sundry tasks that don't seem to be related to looking after the customer or the prospect. It almost feels like busy work.

It is always easiest to do business with people you know, like and trust. So your mission needs to continually focus on the activities that will cause your customers and prospects to know you, like you and trust you. It may be social media, it may be traditional marketing or it may even be contributing to the community. Whatever it is, never lose focus on making sure your customers are looked after and your pipeline is healthy.

By the way, your activities don't have to be major. In fact, it is frequently the little things that make all the difference. The most important thing is to make sure you are doing something.

Let the customer know you are thinking of them and appreciate their business. Let your prospects know you understand their perspective. Ask your customers and prospects what additional products or services they want from you.

It doesn't take a great deal of expense or effort to continue to support your clients and prospects and help them to know you, like you and trust you.

So what are you doing?

# Will You Please Answer the Question?

So often on TV shows that have a courtroom scene, some lawyer will ask a witness a question that then is responded to but not answered. Typically the lawyer interrupts with a very firm, "Will you please answer the question?" Keep this in mind for 11 September.

You see, 11 September is 'R U OK Day'. This has come about because people (particularly men) won't answer the question. We are in the habit of responding to "Are you okay?" with "I'm fine". What most men don't realise is that FINE stands for:

**F** %#ked up,
**I** nsecure,
**N** eurotic and
**E** motional.

We don't like exposing how we are feeling. We carry invisible burdens that only we see and feel (and they are heavy burdens).

For some men, and more and more women, these invisible burdens get so heavy that we get confused. In that confusion suicide seems like a valid option.

The founder of the R U OK organisation, Gavin Larkin, founded it because his successful and gregarious father suicided. Gavin felt that a simple conversation started with the question R U OK would help combat the rising suicide numbers in Australia.

The question R U OK is very important, but not as important as the answer. So, don't forget to ask the question to some of your friends, and if someone asks you the question, answer it! Don't have them feeling like the lawyer shouting "Will you please answer the question!" A problem shared is a problem halved. For those men (typically in senior roles) who are thinking "I couldn't answer the question, it would ruin my reputation, authority, ego" or whatever – this article is dedicated to you.

Will you please answer the question?

**What stops me from feeling OK?**

# Just Keep Swimming

I am having one of those moments. You know those moments? They usually occur just before a breakthrough. They are when you have been doing a lot of work, giving support and resources to others, inspiring those around you, working diligently on your project or focus, but you just don't seem to be getting the traction you want.

A friend once told me, "Don't quit before the miracle happens".

Malcolm Gladwell would say, "Don't quit before the tipping point happens".

Dory would say, "Just keep swimming!"

Shakespeare would say, "Once more unto the breach dear friends".

With these in mind I continue the path. I will look at my obstacles as signposts that I am actually moving forward. No obstacles means I am not doing anything. I have put on loud music that fires me up (thank you Foo Fighters) and I will just keep swimming once more unto the breach and not quit before the tipping point happens as I press on.

I am having one of those moments. Most of us do. They are not good, not bad, they just are.

**How will I move through my down periods?**
_____
_____
_____
_____
_____

# What Can You Throw?

There is a tree just outside my office window. The blossoms are stunning and it is more proof that in the southern hemisphere, spring is upon us. So it must be time for some spring-cleaning.

Not just around the house either. It is a great time to consider your business and place of work. What have you got there that no longer serves you or the business? What have you been thinking of deleting, ejecting, getting rid of, or being free of? What have you been tolerating?

- Maybe it is an employee? If so, make time to start them on a performance improvement plan.
- It could be a process. If so, revisit the process and make it more relevant and effective.
- Your desk may need a tidy up. Put time aside (twice as much as you think you need) and tidy it.
- It may be time to archive some filing. Do a backup and then delete it or have the files put in the archive area.

Whatever it is, it will take time. Book that time in your diary and ask yourself, what can you throw?

**What can I throw?**

_____
_____
_____
_____
_____
_____

# Why Have the Day off?

The first Tuesday in November each year is Melbourne Cup Day. In Australia it is referred to as "the race that stops the nation". In Victoria it is a public holiday. It amazes me that we have a public holiday for a horse race!

Don't get me wrong, a day off appeals to my laidback and relaxed Australian attitude to life, but for a horse race? It also strikes me as funny that in one of the furthest away parts of the Commonwealth, we have a public holiday to celebrate the Queen's birthday, yet they don't have one in England where she lives!

It strikes me as ludicrous that there have been discussions and media rumblings about having a public holiday for the AFL Grand Final (don't get me started on that!).

There are so many good reasons to have a day off where we DON'T; why do it for a simple sporting event?

Here are a few reasons to take a day off, in no order of importance (except the first one):

- Your birthday (NEVER work on your birthday – it's against the rules).
- Your partner's birthday.
- Your anniversary.
- Your child's graduation.
- Your child's performance (sport, play, dance, music, whatever).
- A funeral of someone dear to a dear friend of yours.
- An impulsive family adventure.
- A surprise visit to your grandparents.
- A full health check-up.
- To celebrate a major milestone achievement (personal or professional).

- To spend time with someone you love but don't see often.
- For personal or professional development (training course – regardless of who pays for it).
- To pick up the new car/motorbike/motorhome and spend the day taking it for a test run.
- Because you are sick! (Don't struggle through work; stay home and get better.)
- Because someone you love is sick (kid, pet, partner, parent or friend).

I am sure you can come up with a stack of other reasons far more worthy than a horse race.

So what would it take for you to have the day off?

**I will take a day off for:**
_____
_____
_____
_____
_____
_____

**Now put these dates in your diary!**
_____
_____
_____
_____
_____

# How Sharp is Your Saw?

The 7th habit in Stephen Covey's *7 Habits of Highly Effective People* is "Sharpen the Saw".

What he is saying is how often do you take the time to get better at what you do? Are your skills being improved and honed or are you still doing what you do the same way you always have?

If you were 10% better, what would that mean to you? 10% more sales? 10% better customer service? 10% more time to do things? 10% more organised? 10% more focussed or energised?

Or would it simply mean that you are back to as good as you used to be because you have recently developed some bad habits?

The time you invest in sharpening your saw is well worth it. A saw blade you continue to use slowly gets worn down. It stops sawing and starts hacking. Are you hacking anywhere in your workplace? After you have been hacking for a while, you are then simply going through the motions without getting a result. Surely you aren't simply going through the motions anywhere? Are you?

**How will I sharpen my saw?**
_____
_____
_____
_____
_____
_____
_____

# How Hard is it?

Have you ever had one of those moments where you thought that things were just too hard? Some things in your life had changed and now you couldn't do some of the things that you wanted to?

Maybe you weren't getting the results in your life that you wanted?

It was all too hard?

I have felt that too. Recently I got a sense of perspective. I heard an amazing story from a guy named Dale Elliot. He is a guy just like you and me. No one special – just a bloke with dreams, desires, a life. He took his cousin's motorbike for a spin and on the last corner home a dog ran out onto the road and his life changed forever.

As a paraplegic his life was hard, damn hard!

How does he keep going? By focussing on what he can do, not on what he can't. Looking back to his past and what he can't do serves no purpose. His focus is looking forward at what he can do.

Creating new goals and dreams that stretch him, and doing it with a sense of humour, joy and gratitude.

So how hard is it? Granted, there may be things you can't do like you used to. But what can you do? How can you stretch yourself, grow and make contributions to those around you? I suspect it is easier than you may tell yourself.

# Where is it from?

In today's competitive market, it is easy to lose track of where our supplies come from or even who our suppliers really are. For those of us who are suppliers, this can be scary. All of a sudden, everything is dependent on being the lowest price. But who wants to be a low price supplier? No one wins a price war.

Let me tell you about Sir Francis (and if you are a bit sensitive about animals, you may want to skip to the next paragraph). Sir Francis is our pig, named after Sir Francis Bacon. He was lovingly raised by Lou and Stew from The Farmers Larder. My gorgeous wife and I met Sir Francis and he was a cute little piggy. He is now in our freezer (all 62 kg of him) ready to be invited to dinner. When I tell friends about Sir Francis, some say, "How can you name and pat the pig you will eat?"

If I buy pork at the supermarket, I have no idea where it is from. I have no control over how the pigs were kept or cared for. Knowing my supplier, The Farmers Larder, I KNEW Sir Francis was loved, well cared for and humanely processed. I trusted my supplier to do what was in my best interest as well as theirs. In terms of cost, I was willing to pay whatever they told me (which turned out to be a great price).

Danielle from The Cartridge Family was talking to me about printer paper. I had always used Reflex and was happy with it. She educated me on AA paper and how it was better for the printer for a couple of reasons. Because I have a level of trust with Danielle, I will be switching to AA paper and I am yet to find out the price difference.

If you are a supplier, what are you doing to add value or at the very least, show the existing value to your clients? If your value proposition is strong and proven, price will not be a sticking point.

What about your suppliers? Where do your supplies come from? Is your supplier looking after your needs, not just short-term price but your long-term value? Nowadays, there is ALWAYS a cheaper version (typically from China) but never before has the adage "You get what you pay for" been truer.

**What suppliers do I need to reconsider?**

# Is it Tragic or Magic?

I was thinking of one of my parents' friends. About 15 years ago their daughter (who was 19) was the passenger in a car that had a major accident. Unfortunately their daughter died.

What is more tragic is that her parents stopped a lot of their own life then as well. While their life continued, their focus was on their loss. Whenever they did something or went anywhere, there was always discussion about their daughter.

To me that is tragic. More the loss of their life than the loss of their daughter's.

Life is full of bad things happening to good people. The question that is the biggest waste of time and energy is, "Why?" In my experience, you will never get an answer that satisfies you. There is always a further why. The healthiest question is, "What can I do about it?" This gives you a course of action and a way forward.

Is your life tragic or magic?

For most of us, it can be either. It is completely dependent on your perspective. Take my own life. I could easily look at it as being quite tragic.

- I grew up in a small country town where I didn't drink or play sport so I never "fitted in".
- Just as I was in my formative years I got sent to a school 90 minutes away on the bus.
- It took me 12 months to settle in to the new school and make friends.
- It was too far away to have friends over after school so I couldn't consolidate my friendships.
- I had to work on the farm and regularly cook for a family of five.
- We had a massive vegetable garden and I had to maintain it.

- I didn't know what I wanted to be when I grew up so I "fell" into a uni course I wasn't keen on.

Or it could be magic:

- I grew up in a country town so I got to breathe fresh air and see the stars at night. It also gave me a friendly approach to people and an ability to talk to anyone.
- I was fortunate enough to go to a school with a high academic standard to set me up with a top-class education.
- Having friends from all over the place enabled me to get some varied perspectives on life.
- I learnt to cook at a young age and could handle catering for larger numbers with ease.
- While I lived at home I ate organic vegetables without realising such a thing existed – I just called them vegetables!
- I didn't know what I wanted to do after school so I took on a double degree to give me options for the future.

Zig Ziglar said that our attitude determines our altitude. Tragedies will strike, challenges will be faced, terrible things will happen to fabulous people and life will go on. It is up to us as individuals whether we see it as tragic or magic.

How do you see your life and your world? Is it tragic or magic?

**How do I see my life?**
_____
_____
_____
_____
_____

# What Do Little Old Ladies Know?

Too often we dismiss the little old lady. They look frail, mind their own business and get on with life. But I believe we can learn a lot from them.

As I was leaving the NSAA presidential breakfast with my vice president, we saw a large semitrailer seemingly stuck in a car park at a shopping centre. It had hit the "too high" bar and the driver was busy on the phone trying to work out what to do. The little old lady knew what to do.

Several drivers impatiently drove their car on the wrong side of the road to get around the truck. Other pedestrians, shuffled around avoiding everyone, but the little old lady knew what to do!

She gracefully and with purpose went about her business walking toward the shops. As she crossed the road in front of the truck (whose driver was still on the phone) she gave him a big wave to say "Thanks for stopping for me".

The vice president and I cracked up laughing as it looked so comical. But that was when I realised that the little old lady was right.

Regardless of whether the truck had stopped for her or not, she waved a thank you as if it did. She was courteous, graceful and focussed on what she needed to achieve for the day while realising that sometimes you will get support from unexpected places. Even if it is merely a truck that has stopped where you need it to.

Too often the youth of today (and those who still wish they were the youth of today!) dismiss out of hand the lessons from those who have had more life experience. Today I got one from a little old lady just living her life.

One of my favourite little old ladies, Betty White, gave her Ten Tips for Living a Long and Happy Life on the Letterman show.

Here are some of my favourites from Betty:

- Get at least eight hours of beauty sleep, nine if you are ugly.
- Avoid tweeting any photos of your private parts.
- Schedule a nightly appointment with Johnny Walker.
- Don't waste your time watching TV.
- Never dwell on past mistakes.
- Try not to die.

What can you learn from the little old ladies in your life?

**What lessons can I learn from more experienced people?**

# THERE IS NO LUCK

I was away with five of my friends and a couple of their kids for a four-day weekend at Mt Buller.

Some of you may be thinking, "How lucky".

There is no luck.

Rather than spend a lot of money on a holiday house and then have to spend each visit there doing maintenance, the six of us have formed a B&B consortium. We all put $50 a month into the B&B fund and then every couple of months we go away for an extended weekend. Not bad having a magic little break away all for less than a cup of coffee a day. No maintenance, no bills, no hassle just pure holiday bliss.

I have always believed that holidays (or a new car or a new piece of equipment or a new whatever you want) are not dependant on luck. They only take two things: planning and cash. If your planning is good enough, you don't really need to worry about the cash.

So what do you want? What will you do to make sure that luck plays no part in whether you get it or not? It just takes two things:

Planning and cash.

**When will I take my next holiday?**
_____
_____
_____
_____
_____

# What's the Risk?

Every year the choir that I sing with, Mood Swing, perform at a memorial service for people who have died in the workplace. It is always a privilege to be part of this service and always disturbing to realise how fragile life is.

It made me think of the risks that people take in the workplace. I have seen tradespeople working on a roof without safety barriers or safety harness. As a kid I recall jumping on and off moving tractors while feeding out hay. Plenty of people in offices have stood on swivel chairs with no support as they reach for something on top of the cabinet. Some of the risks we take can have severe consequences, but we take the risk anyway without thinking about it.

When it comes to financial risk, we are usually vigilant about minimising it. When it comes to our health and state of being, we seem to be willing to take significant risks. Don't get me wrong, I am not saying "NEVER take a risk"; I am saying "minimise and manage your risks". A life without risks is restrictive and detrimental, but taking unnecessary risks is foolish.

So in what you are doing, what's the risk? More importantly, how will you manage it and minimise it?

**Where is my risk?**

_____
_____
_____
_____
_____
_____
_____

# How are Your Relationships?

I interviewed Yvonne Allen, founder of Australia's most successful dating agency. As you would expect, our topic was relationships. Not just intimate relationships, but working relationships, friend relationships and even relationships with service providers.

It will come as no surprise to you to know that many of our relationships are suffering. While there is a large "man drought" for 25 to 45-year-old women, there is also a lot of confusion around how to act and react. Yvonne refers to this as the "gender agenda". We seem to have a lot of confusion out there. Women who are told to be more like men to succeed and men who are told to be more like women to understand them. No wonder there is confusion!

Yvonne's tips for relationship success include:

- Start with the relationship you have with yourself and make sure it is healthy.
- Consider what the other person in the relationship (or you) wants and is looking for.
- Focus on the positives of the relationship.
- Communicate so that everyone knows exactly where they stand without having to read minds.
- Commit to the relationship so that it can grow in depth rather than ending at the first sign of trouble.

When Yvonne was talking I couldn't help but notice that these points are exactly what business needs as well. Think about your team, your suppliers, your direct reports, your boss, your customers, your friends and your family. Would applying Yvonne's tips help any of them?

So how are your relationships?

# The Phone Call

Never forget the importance of a follow-up phone call. If you are thinking about a client, prospect or friend, chances are they are thinking about you or they need you for their business problem.

Call them because thinking about them is just not enough!

I just called a prospect I had sent a proposal to a couple of weeks ago. I asked if he had any thoughts and he said it was all straightforward and he is just waiting to speak to the boss.

I feel better as I know my contact is keen, he now knows I care enough to check if he has questions and it is also a reminder for him to follow up with his boss.

All that in one quick phone call.

**I need to call:**

# IS YOUR REWARD RELEVANT?

I believe we need to let people in our team (including suppliers, customers and family) know how much we value them and their contribution. Too often we just assume they know we appreciate what they do. As you get in the habit of rewarding people, make sure it is relevant.

A financial bonus typically has minimal impact because how much is enough? No matter how much a person receives, they always have that small thought in the back of their head "Is that it?" One of my clients has stopped issuing movie tickets as they have given away so many, they no longer mean anything. You have to make the reward relevant and it doesn't have to cost too much!

I did two lots of Santa work for a friend of mine. I was happy to do it and it was a lot of fun. To say thanks he unexpectedly gave me a trophy. It was incredibly relevant and a load of fun. Will I do it again if he asks me? You bet I will.

I probably would have anyway, but a cool gift like this means it would be nearly impossible to say no.

What rewards or gifts are you giving those in your team?

Is your reward relevant?

**What rewards will inspire my team?**
_____
_____
_____
_____
_____

122 | GET MORE INSPIRATION

# Humans Can't See

Humans MUST be admired for their commitment to selective blindness and ignorance. They KNOW what is in their best interest yet they continue to ignore it and pretend that their situation is different.

It started with dog poo.

Dog owners are typically responsible and pick up after their animals as required by law, but there are a minority (or is it a silent majority) that CANNOT notice their dog bearing down to squeeze out a nugget.

Surely the human must notice the tension on the lead or strange circling behaviour of their pet, but it always seems to be at that time that the human gets in touch with their ornithology gene and starts bird-watching. This leaves the nugget on the footpath or nature strip of some unsuspecting homeowner to be flung around when next the lawn is mowed.

Even worse, it could be at the park where "everyone does it – so it must be okay". It is not okay. Ask any amateur sportsperson who has slid through it, stomped on it, hit it, fallen in it or kicked it and see what they think of it. Ask any pram-pushing parent how they felt when they got the pram in the car only to discover their new aromatherapy was Eau de Puppy.

You would have thought we would have learnt.

By now you may be thinking either "Oops I've done that" or "It's a disgrace, damn dog owners". If you are one of the latter, when was the last time you chucked something out the window of a moving car, put a non-recyclable in the recycling bin, put a recyclable in the non-recycling bin or threw some foreign object in a waterway?

In Ye Olde England, humans just lobbed the bath water and chamber pot out the window. Over the years this slowly changed to open sewers (pumped straight into the river) to closed sewers (still pumped into the river) and now finally we have some decent sewerage processing that can turn our waste into pure water and by-product.

You would have thought we would have learnt.

We now have expeditions that are hiking up Mount Everest purely to collect the rubbish. From empty oxygen cylinders to dead bodies, we continue to leave our waste in some of the most pristine areas. There is so much space junk orbiting the earth that it is starting to damage satellites and there are high-level discussions to do a rubbish collection space run.

You would have thought we would have learnt.

The younger generations seem to be more accustomed to considering the full impact of their actions, but there are exceptions. The more mature generations, who run most of our corporations, are less likely to consider the impact of their actions and those of their companies than the impact on their bottom line.

What is needed is RESPONSIBILITY. That equates to the "ability to respond". It is not fun to pick up dog poo, especially if you have a big dog. But if you choose to own a dog, part of the deal is looking after it. It is not fun to correct the environmental and social impact of your business, but that is part of the responsibility of running a business.

Humans MUST be admired for their commitment to selective blindness and ignorance. They KNOW what is in their best interest yet they continue to ignore it and pretend that their situation is different.

**Where do I need to take responsibility?**

# What About this Weather?

Whew! It was a SCORCHER here in Melbourne – 40 C.

I could whinge and whine about how hot it is. I could complain that I don't deal with the heat well. Just so you know, I am a son of a farmer so I know how to complain about the weather like a professional!

The weather is something I can do nothing about.

The saying "It's not what happens to you but how you deal with it that counts" is best represented by the weather.

In business it may be that your main customer no longer buys from you, your key employee resigns, someone else owns a trademark you were after or some other unfortunate event.

So today, I am not going to say anything about the weather. I will simply do what it takes to make sure my needs are met. It could be going to the cinema, it may be working out of an air-conditioned café, I may even need to go and hang out in the freezer section of a supermarket.

It is the action I take that will determine how well I deal with my situation.

**What action do I need to take TODAY?**
_____
_____
_____
_____
_____

# What About the Little Guys?

Recently I have been on three different airlines: Qantas, REX and Jetstar. The service I got varied with each one.

More importantly, it varied against my expectations.

The first flight was Qantas. To make things easier for them they now have auto-baggage check-in. In fact, it is okay for the traveller too, unless you have unusual luggage. I had a guitar with me. The auto check-in wanted to charge me an extra $30 as I had an extra bag. I spoke to the assistant (when I could find her) and had a conversation about luggage and what was allowed in the cabin. This was from the premium airline. I had 25 kg allocation and still I was hassled.

Compare that to REX airlines. When I booked I noticed that the luggage allowance was 15 kg. I knew I would be over the limit with the guitar, amp and other things I had, so I rang them to try and buy more luggage allowance, as it is usually cheaper to buy beforehand than at the airport. I was advised that I could only get it at the airport. I steeled myself for the $5.50 per kilo extra I would have to pay (I guessed about $40) and then checked in when I was in Sydney. At check-in the bag and guitar weighed a total of 22.5 kg.

As I waited to be told "That's $40 please" he actually said, "Let's say that's 20 kg and there is no extra charge. By the way, would you like an exit row? It would be more comfortable for a guy your height." I was stunned.

In an age where the focus is on cost-cutting and the bottom line (particularly in the airline industry), it was a delight to get great service. This service continued on the flight – but that's another story.

# Have You Exercised Your Slack Muscle?

My gorgeous wife and I are into investment properties. We like them and they work for us.

Late last year a tenant advised us that someone had broken in and done some damage. It turned out the damage was smashed walls, windows and a massive mess. The neighbours advised us that within weeks of moving in there was a huge party and the cops had to be called. In fact, the party made the local paper.

Personally, I suspect the damage was more "party" related than "break-in" related.

Anyway, the landlord insurance covered the replastering of a third of the house and we took the opportunity to repaint the entire inside of the house and re-carpet it. That is not us hiring painters, that is my gorgeous wife and I spending three 14-hour days washing ceilings and walls and then giving the ceilings, walls, door frames and doors two coats of paint.

To be honest, I was physically shattered!

I am used to speaking on stage, strutting around trade shows, talking on the phone or working at my computer. I have all these muscles that had gone slack in my body. An intense painting workout reminded me they were still there.

It got me thinking about some of the muscles I used to exercise in the workplace but haven't for a while. I haven't done cold calling for quite a while, I haven't done random networking for a while and I haven't called my old clients to see how they are for a while.

Like my slack painting muscles, when I do this it may feel strange, hurt a bit, make me feel exhausted or even turn me off doing it ever again. It is so important to exercise the slack muscle in your business. To do the tasks that pay off, even if you don't want to do them.

Have you exercised your slack muscle recently?

**I need to exercise these slack muscles:**

# What is Your Backup Plan?

When everything is going fine, we don't spend time thinking about what could go wrong. But it is when everything is going fine that you MUST consider what happens if things go wrong?

My gorgeous wife and I were out for lunch with friends celebrating my gorgeous wife's birthday. It was a lovely place in the Yarra Valley wine region. A hot (33 °C) and windy day, but comfy in the air-conditioned restaurant.

Then the power went out.

As they have electric doors, the first response is that the doors automatically open. This let in the blustery warm wind. We ordered food and were told that they couldn't start cooking it yet.

One of our party went to the toilet and came back quickly saying there were no lights in there.

Fortunately they had a backup generator so after a little bit, the power came back on and all was okay. Then just as our meal was served the power went off again (doors opened again too!). This time it didn't come back on. After dessert, a waitress came over to ask us what we had so she could prepare the bill.

Essentially they had a backup plan, but not a secondary backup plan. It seemed that their generator had enough capacity to help shut things down, but not enough to run their operations on an ongoing basis.

What about your business?
What would you do if your power was out for the day?
What would you do if your computer hard drive crashed?
What would you do if you could not issue invoices?

Now is the time to have a plan in place and then follow it when you need to.

So what is your backup plan?

**This is my backup plan:**

# How are Your Reflexes?

Can you twist, turn and flip when you need to?

I was riding my motorbike to a client site for some mentoring (yes my motorbike is my company vehicle! Yay!). On the way two people nearly killed me and a police officer nearly scared me to death.

The two drivers didn't mean to nearly kill me, they just changed lanes without looking properly. It's easy to do; I have done it myself. Fortunately, every time I go out on the bike I expect someone to do this so I am hypervigilant. On both occasions I could quickly twist the bike out of harm's way.

The police officer scared me because he sounded his siren for a burst. I knew he was behind me, but I didn't notice the unmarked police car to his left. He was basically saying "hello" to his mate, police style. As soon as I saw the unmarked car I knew I had nothing to worry about.

Running or working in a business is the same. You have to be alert (but not alarmed) for things that may cause damage to your business or cause you to go in another direction. When you detect these you need to be willing to quickly change direction. You also need to be alert for things that sound and look like they need a reaction, but don't.

So how are your reflexes? Can you twist, turn and flip in your business when you need to?

**How do I stay alert?**

# Is Your Body Where it Needs to be?

The late, great Kevin Merry (my dad) often said to me, "Sometimes your body just has to be there whether you want to go or not". Usually he was talking about funerals, weddings, celebrations and events where you could choose to go or not.

That message always stuck with me. It was reinforced when I missed one of my best friend's weddings – a decision I will always regret. (Sorry Simon.)

But I am one who learns from mistakes. So my gorgeous wife and I went to her friend's wedding. It was an Indian wedding in India. In fact, it was a Punjabi Sikh wedding so that meant four days of celebration spread over a week. I even grew a beard for the occasion to go with my turban!

Three weeks out of my business was not really what I had planned. It set me back on a few things, but my gorgeous wife and I decided that our bodies had to be there. The bridal couple are fabulous people, it was an amazing cultural experience, we got to spend a little extra time enjoying the delights of India and I didn't have to shave for a month. So many great reasons to be there. If I really wanted, I could have come up with many reasons why it would have been better to be at home.

Sometimes your body just has to be there.

# Are You Working Right?

I was working with a mentoring client and telling her that she needs to do less and less to achieve more and more. Yes, yes, this seems silly at first glance, but it is the secret to success (well one of them anyway).

Look at the most senior person in any organisation. Essentially they do nothing. Don't get me wrong, they are busy, but they do nothing. Their day consists of meetings, phone calls, and checking things. They have learnt the secret of getting their people to do the work and they just make sure the right things get done at the right time.

What about you?

Now you may say "Oh, but I am just a solopreneur" or "a mere employee", but the same principle applies. It may be that you get colleagues to do the work or outsource it to a virtual assistant or third party.

You can achieve more by doing less. Your value is in knowing what needs to be done, when it needs to be done and who is the best person to do it. The person who thinks "No one can do it as well as me" is the one working massive hours and feeling exhausted.

So are you working right?

What can you delegate or outsource?

**What will I delegate today?**
_____
_____
_____
_____

# How Do You Recover?

Customer service is important but don't forget your service recovery skills either. Research shows that a customer who has a good experience will tell three to five people, but a customer who has a bad experience will tell 11 people and now with social media, I suspect it's more.

Recently I was away with our B&B group of seven people.

We had booked a large and lovely place in Echuca with additional bungalow. We arranged and paid for it all over the internet before arrival. When we arrived at the booking agent we found that it was an additional $150 for the bungalow in addition to the $1,000 we had already paid even though this had not been advertised anywhere.

I raised this with the booking agent who happened to be the owner.

Some of her comments included, "We have never had this problem before", "My team know what they are doing, I am sure they would have mentioned it", "I wasn't part of your original conversation so I can't know for sure what was said". At the end of the day, she had a very unhappy customer and she did not care.

There are many things that she could have done, at the very least acknowledging the emotive side of the transaction. While she may have got her $150, she won't get any further business or recommendations from the seven of us who were there and she won't get positive comments on her website.

So how do you recover?

# Can They Hear You?

Too many people in this world keep their light hidden. They have thoughts, ideas, dreams, contributions, VALUE that they do not share.

Why?

Who knows? It could be intimidation, lack of self-worth, shyness, being overlooked; for whatever reasons, their voice is not heard.

You HAVE to speak up.

What you have to offer the world is too important to keep to yourself. If you can't speak up, find a way. Write something, do something, paint something, raise your hand, do whatever you need to do to be heard.

**Where do I need to speak up?**

# What's Your Why?

In presentations and discussions with clients, there are a lot of discussions about people's "why". It can be challenging enough to keep yourself continually focussed and on track, let alone your team.

The thing that will do that is your "why".

So why do you do what you do? Is it:

- To make $1,000,000
- Because the boss said so
- To provide for my kids
- To ski the Alps of Europe
- I don't know what else I can do
- To get a hot sports car
- To achieve inner peace
- It's what I have always done
- Because I want to retire at 50

Whatever the reason, HAVE a reason. Have a POSITIVE and attractive reason. Get a target for yourself that you really want to achieve. So many people are not inspired by their work purely because they do not know their "why".

**What's my why?**
_____
_____
_____
_____
_____

# Have You Broken the Habit?

After a month of travelling, a couple of weeks of "man flu" (it was tragic) and a couple of weeks of pretty average excuses, I finally got my body back to my personal trainer.

I have to say, those first two sessions nearly killed me – but they hurt more the next day.

It is a bit like the habits you have around the house and around your workplace. They are so much easier to break than they are to make. Yet once you get into them, they seem to have a life of their own.

Be it making daily sales calls, writing daily blogs, keeping yourself OFF Facebook, regular walks around the team to check how they are or simply putting the rubbish out when you need to, maintaining the focus on your habit and its outcome is far easier than breaking the habit and starting again.

What habits are you willing to maintain today or have you broken the habit?

**What habits do I need to keep?**

# Got Synergy?

John Donne, a 17th-century English author famously said, "No man is an island". Then why do so many of us try and deal with our businesses, our lives and challenging situations on our own?

I have been to several weddings where the celebrant says, "A problem shared is a problem halved" or "A joy shared is a joy doubled" and still we don't get it.

Synergy is where the energy from the whole is greater than the energy from the sum of its parts. To maximise the synergy, the part has to truly commit itself to the process. For us, that means we have to be willing to be vulnerable, to listen, to be accepting, to share, to wish the best for each other.

I recently had one of the most amazing, synergistic weekends from a personal and professional point of view. My belief is I got so much out of it because I was willing to put all of myself into it.

Have you got synergy? If not, what are you willing to do to get it?

**How will I get more synergy?**
_____
_____
_____
_____
_____
_____
_____
_____

# Can You Make it Easy?

I am stunned by the way so many stores make it hard to be a client.

Myer seems to have fewer and fewer service assistants. It is not uncommon to have to walk a big chunk of the floor to find someone to help you, let alone a person at a register to help you buy the item.

Coles and Woolworths have put in new self-serve checkouts all over the place. It saves them a lot of staffing costs. While some of us techno-friendly people love it, I have seen non-techno people tormented by them and the assistant not be able to tolerate the customer not getting it.

What about for us as home-based businesses, how do we make it hard for people to be our customers?

I love to buy resources off the internet, but if it is a multi-stage process, it just gets too hard. If I have to re-enter the same information over and over again, I have cancelled sales. I find it very annoying to enter all my details and then be sent to PayPal or some other payment gateway and have to enter them again. It is a lost sale if I like what you have and then have to ring between the hours of 10.00 am and 2.00 pm to order it over the phone. At trade shows, if we make people fill out forms to enter a prize rather than just put their business card in a bowl, we can miss a prospect.

Are you getting the idea?

Too many sles are lost or prospects missed because we are considering what makes things easy for me and not for you.

The cracker is ordering movie tickets online from Village. They spend a lot of effort telling people how easy it is to order online or on your phone. No waiting in line, pick your own seat, all nice and easy. Yet when you go to do it, there is an additional fee of around $2 for each ticket you buy online. Why would you do that? To my mind, having people order online or on the phone would save staff costs, paper cost (no issue of tickets) and increase customer satisfaction. I would make it $1 cheaper and people would flock to it. Plus you would then get their ordering details and you could directly market to them. Surely that is worth something?

So how can you make it easy for your customers to deal with you?

Here are some thoughts:

- Accept credit cards.
- Give a rock solid guarantee (mine is a 200% money back guarantee).
- Have a single step checkout.
- Smile when dealing with customers.
- Have accurate signage (don't laugh, some business signage is ridiculous).
- Under promise and over deliver.
- You pay the postage (increase the price to cover it if you need).

**What will I do?**

# Are You Adding Value?

A while ago I was on the lovely Gold Coast of Australia. I was there for a client's conference and expo. They asked me to host the expo floor and work closely with the exhibitors. Naturally I said yes.

Then they said, "Would you mind dressing up for the welcoming function?" I thought they meant dressing up in a formal outfit.

But no, my ob was to be outside the confessional (photo booth) and absolve people of their sins dressed as a religious figure. I am sure I could have said no. But my theory is always to look for how I can add value to my clients. What can I do that is one step further? Not only does it make them happy, it also means I am more likely to get the gig again next year.

So how are you adding value? It doesn't mean simply dressing up or working longer hours. What are the things you are doing for your customers (both internal and external) that add value to them and make their experience more enjoyable?

**How can I add value to my customers?**
_____
_____
_____
_____
_____
_____
_____
_____
_____

# Are You Flexible?

OMG! Can you believe it? I stuffed up.

I live in Melbourne and didn't realise that I had scheduled my *How to Create and Deliver a Great Introduction* webinar smack bang in the middle of Melbourne Cup Day. Naturally I only found out about this just after I had sent the newsletter to over 1,500 people!

So a few quick tinkerings of the system and voila, the time was changed.

What about you? When you find out about a problem can you let go of control enough to be flexible? Can you release the idea of what you wanted to happen and come up with a solution that will suit? From a cancelled meeting to a cancelled contract, anything can happen. As has been said so many times, it is not what happens to you but how you deal with it that counts.

So are you flexible enough to deal with what happens to you?

**How can I be more flexible?**

# Are You Protecting Your Assets?

In business and life it is important to protect your assets. Sometimes our most important assets are not "things" but "skills".

For example, as a Master of Ceremonies and Event Strategist, my most important asset is my ability to talk. Unfortunately I did not protect that asset and I lost my voice! (The good news is that for the first time in a long time, my gorgeous wife could finish her own sentences without me interrupting!)

I was speaking at a gig – it was pretty warm and I was drinking ice water before I spoke. At the end my voice was a little strained but I thought it would recover. I was then MC at a wedding. I had spent the day chatting with a friend who had come down from Queensland and then the wedding venue was noisy so I had to shout to talk.

The PA was poor quality so I strained the strain. As you may expect, the best thing to do is to not talk and let it recover. But my gorgeous wife and I had lunch and dinner planned with two sets of friends the next day. I tried not to talk but I can't help myself.

Result: I had a very sore throat and minimal voice. This all started with the ice water. If you are a performer, you must only drink room temperature water as it keeps your vocal chords flexible and ready to work. I know this but still I did not protect my assets.

What about you?

What assets do you need to protect?

How will you do that?

# Are You Trained?

I regularly spend three days locked in a room with other similar minded entrepreneurs. Well maybe not locked, but you get what I mean. We were looking at how to transform our businesses and take them to the next level (or even the one beyond that). The final day was planning and commitments for the year ahead with an action plan to help get us there.

As a business owner it can be hard to dedicate this kind of time for additional training and development.

As an employee as well, there is always too much to do to spend time off getting training and development.

I have heard it said by many business gurus, "Too many managers say 'What if I train my employees and they leave', but what if you don't train them and they stay!"

By the way, don't wait for others to pay for or approve your training either. If you really want it or need it, be prepared to finance it yourself, after all, you get to keep it!

So what training do you need? What skills do you need to develop?

What will you do TODAY to make that happen?

**What further development do I need?**
_____
_____
_____
_____
_____

# How Good is Your Call to Action?

I spoke to a school group recently. On the way there I saw a delivery van covered with signage about their products. There was lots of colour and pictures, but the sign that stood out were words saying:

"Book with me now!"

My initial response was "Book what?"

You see, their signage got attention, but you could not tell at a glance what it was for. With signage on a vehicle that moves at somewhere between 40 and 100 km/h you have to be able to understand it in a single glance.

This is a principle that I share with clients in my exhibiting work.

Can you tell at a glance what your stand is about?

It is equally applicable to the action line on an email. If the recipient cannot understand what you want from them at a glance, then you need to rework your call to action.

Are you getting the response you want with your "call to action?"

**What call to actions do I need?**
_____
_____
_____
_____
_____

# Do Your Systems Support You?

Do your systems support you? I am not just talking about computer systems, but your manual systems and processes as well.

Michael Gerber is the king of business systems. His book, *The E-Myth Revisited*, has some simple yet masterful comments and ideas on how you let your systems run the business and your people run the systems.

So how can you systemise more? From the simple addition of checklists on order forms, to a weekly structure for your time, or simply having custom lead cards to collect a prospect's details when you next exhibit or are sponsoring an event. The systems make your job easier and free you up for more strategic work (or holidays!).

So do your systems support you?

**Do my systems support me?**
_____
_____
_____
_____
_____
_____
_____
_____
_____
_____

# What Do You Want?

I have long been of the opinion that you get what you ask for not what you deserve.

Sometimes when people on the street ask for money I will say:

"How much do you want?"

If they ask for $2 it is what I give them. If it is $20, that is what they get.

I came across some footage that validates my theory. At a Q&A session with Billy Joel at Vanderbilt University, student Michael Pollack asked the question, "Can I accompany you singing 'New York State of Mind'?"

The answer was, "Yes".

So remember, one of the keys to success is to keep asking for whatever you want.

Ask away!

**What do I want?**
_____
_____
_____
_____
_____
_____
_____
_____
_____

# WHAT DO YOU THINK?

I love Henry Ford's quote:

"Whether you think you can or think you can't, you're right!"

Sometimes I find I know I can, but some doubts sneak in around the edges. Things are not happening the way I planned, I am not getting the results I want or I have lost my serenity about my place in the world and self-doubt comes in. When this happens I turn on loud, up-tempo music, look at the lovely client comments in my "happy file" and keep putting one foot forward and taking some kind of action.

What do you do?

What is your strategy to keep your head on straight and your confidence high?

**What will I do to stay positive?**

# Things are Changing

The only constant is change.

We have read that, heard that and seen that so many times, yet still change surprises us. I was speaking to a large management team about change (among other things) and they proudly told me that they all embrace change.

Upon further investigation, it turns out most of them ALWAYS sleep on the same side of the bed, have THEIR CHAIR at the dining table and in the lounge room and when they go to the monthly meeting they nearly always sit in the same spot. That doesn't mean they are no good at change, but it may mean that they struggle to embrace change more than they think.

What about you? How are you with change?

**How will I embrace change?**
___
___
___
___
___
___
___
___
___
___
___
___

# Does it Hurt?

Recently my gorgeous wife and I cooked up a Sri Lankan curry feast for a group of friends. One couple brought their ten and 14-year-old kids with them. Now my gorgeous wife and I like a bit of kick in our curries and even though we tried to make tame ones, a couple of them were a bit strong.

Our friends' ten-year-old had never had authentic curry. He was keen to try something new. Now we warned him that some were a bit hot and if it was too hot to have some yoghurt or a banana (water really doesn't help). So he knew it could cause him some pain but he wanted to try anyway. He started on the potato curry, which was the really hot one. A few tears welled up, his face turned red and he went for the yoghurt big time. But he also kept his good humour and then went for some cooler and less spicy foods.

A great effort and kudos to him.

What about you? When did you last try something new?

Something you knew had the potential to cause you pain as well as representing a milestone in new experiences? When did you last ask "Does it hurt?" and even when the answer is "yes" or "maybe" do it anyway?

**What "new" things will I do?**
_____
_____
_____
_____
_____
_____
_____

# Have You Got a Card?

I was at a friend's birthday party. It was a fantastic event and I was sitting with some people I had never met before. Now as usual, we started talking about what we did. It's a standard opener, "So what do you do?" You have probably used it yourself.

Well it didn't take long until we were chatting away full steam and were coming up with ideas on how to increase her business. It only made sense after talking business to ask for her business card and give her one of mine.

Then I shuffled seats. Again the conversation started, "So what do you do?" And we were off and racing (in fact, he is into horses and runs a horse magazine). A few more ideas and then it was "So do you have a business card?"

If you are like me and are passionate about what you do and how you may be able to help others, why wouldn't you give a business card? Much to my gorgeous wife's dismay, I have even swapped business cards at a funeral!

Now while you probably don't need them as much now as you can put details in your phone, it is always great to have them handy. (I am often surprised at people who go to networking events without a stack of business cards. What the?) I was taught years ago that a business card in your wallet gets crushed. So I have a stash of them in the special pocket of each suit jacket, the glove box of the car, my compendium, my cardholder and some reserve in my wallet. It pays to be ready if ever someone asks, "So what do you do?" or "Have you got a card?"

**Where will I keep my business cards?**
_____
_____
_____
_____

# WHAT HAVEN'T YOU SAID?

I had misinterpreted a client's email. You know when you put meaning in an email that isn't there? So I didn't get in touch.

... Time passed ...

Now whenever I thought of the client I started thinking, "I really should give them a call".

... Time passed ...

I found great ways to side-track myself from the call and now it was six months later so I put some backstop methods in place to be sure I called.

- I called.
- Then I visited and took responsibility for my stuff.
- The client then signed up for more of my services (they had been waiting for me to call!).

Whether it is a client you haven't called, a friend you haven't spoken to or a loved one you need to say something to, don't leave it unsaid. The rewards and peace of mind will ALWAYS outweigh the discomfort.

So what haven't you said?

**Who do I need to talk to today?**
_____
_____
_____
_____
_____
_____

# Do You Communicate Both Ways?

With my Executive Mentoring clients, there is a common complaint that their teams don't listen to them and they can't understand why.

My experience has shown that your team are more likely to listen to you if you listen to them first. The basic rule of communication is "You have two ears and one mouth, use them in that ratio".

What about your team and your colleagues, do you listen to them?

You don't have to agree with them but do you listen to them?

Again, I am not talking about just hearing them but actually listening to them. I KNOW it feels like it takes more effort, but the reality is with more clarity in your communication there is a reduced need for repeat communication so it actually saves time.

So do you communicate both ways?

**Who do I need to listen to?**
_____
_____
_____
_____
_____
_____
_____

# WHAT'S HAPPENING?

Of late, many of my clients keep talking about how busy they are, which is a great thing. But what is actually happening?

Too often people will get caught up in a "groundhog day" type of cycle. You know the one – you wake up, go to work, come home late, say hi to your family, have dinner, watch TV, go to bed and wake up, go to work ... and so on.

With the new, ever invasive technology it is getting worse. Emails are ALWAYS available. Work resources are now accessible everywhere.

There is no OFF switch.

I have long been a believer in having a hobby. Something you do to give you energy, excitement and a connection with others.

Something that feeds your soul. Do you have one?

My friend and business collaborator Tanya is many things, and singing is one of her hobbies. My gorgeous wife and I were privileged to see Tanya and her class graduate from a jazz singing intensive at the Paris Cat Jazz Club (in Melbourne). There were some great performances, some nervous performances, some shaky performances, but they gave their best and it was pretty good. Most importantly, the energy of achieving something for themselves in front of a crowd of 60 people was bubbling around us.

When was the last time you felt that way? So, for you, what's happening?

# Fanfare for the Common Man

During the course of a weekend, my gorgeous wife and I did a road trip to Ballarat. A cruisey two-hour drive. Serendipitously we ended up at the art gallery and were delighted by an exhibition of works by Robert Clinch. His works were stunning.

We were thrilled to see some of the detail in his studies for the final pieces, tickled by the play on words of the names of his pieces and impressed by the way the gallery had displayed them to highlight their features.

Frequently, as the title of the exhibition (and of this article) convey, they celebrated the common things in life. The simple act of playing a trombone, a truck being loaded at the docks, the monolithical creation of a warehouse and paper planes.

What are the seemingly ordinary and common things in your life you wish to celebrate? The writing of a letter to a friend, maybe taking a dog for a walk or even the simple joy of rain pouring down making magical music. Sometimes it is not just the extraordinary that needs to be celebrated, but the average, everyday, mundane and seemingly boring things that make life worthwhile.

What will you celebrate with a "fanfare for the common man" (and woman)?

**What can I start RIGHT NOW?**
_____
_____
_____
_____

# How Big is Your Bite?

"Don't bite off more than you can chew!" I think every mother has said that to her child at some time. Many managers have also said or heard it.

Kerry Packer once said, "Take a big bite and chew like mad" (or words to that effect).

What about you? How big is your bite? Do you relish the risk of taking on too much or do you manage your resources well?

The important thing to remember is that no matter how big your bite, whatever you do will have an impact. Make sure you can deal with the impact and consequences of your action.

**Where do I need to take a "big bite"?**

# What are You Waiting for?

Too often we wait for the right time, the right weather, the right signs, the right ... (fill in the blank).

Don't wait!

It is just another excuse to delay, consider, ponder, avoid and suffer. The time will never be "just right". Sometimes you just have to stand up and take action to get the results. Sure, it may not be perfect but it is better than nothing.

So what are you waiting for?

**What Can I Start RIGHT NOW?**
_____
_____
_____
_____
_____
_____
_____
_____
_____
_____
_____
_____
_____

# What Counts?

It is very easy to get hooked up on the material things. It is easy to get swept up in the loop of "must make money, must save money, must spend money".

So what really counts?

The answer is different for everyone and sometimes the answer doesn't present itself until much later in life.

I would strongly suggest to you that money is only one way to measure what counts and there are a plethora of other ways. Living in the country, running your own business, being creative, singing to an audience, having a family, creating a garden, being an active member of the community, being a person of faith, laughing with friends, learning new skills, reading, travelling, caring for others, your fitness, owning your own home, sharing your own home, sharing someone else's home ... there is no end to the list.

What is important is to decide for yourself what really counts and then pursue it regardless of what others say.

**What counts?**
_____
_____
_____
_____
_____
_____
_____
_____

# Got Leverage?

Archimedes (the mathematical legend) said something to the effect of, "Give me a lever long enough ... and I shall move the world".

This principle remains valid today in engineering as well as in finance and in business.

Today our levers are not simply a large plank of wood. They can be leveraging the ideas and wisdom of others as well as the finance of others. It is one of the many reasons why my gorgeous wife and I love investing in property. We can get some excellent leverage financially and from others' experience.

While we are living in one of the most affluent of times and the quality of life that most of us experience has never been higher, I believe it is still important to plan for the future. I am in the age group where I will not have a pension available. Laws on superannuation keep changing for seemingly political reasons. So I am using leverage NOW to build a better future.

What about you?

Are you taking advantage of the leverage available to you? Are you fast-tracking your skillsets by learning from others? Are you using your finance in an intelligent way to maximise its growth?

Quite simply, have you got leverage?

**Where do I need more leverage?**
_____
_____
_____
_____
_____

# Your Skills Don't Count

That may be hard to accept, but there are so many people out there with unbelievable skills that have not experienced the level of success that they are after.

What counts more than your skillset, is your attitude.

Working with my consulting clients who are looking to employ people, I always advise them to hire on attitude as you can teach anyone a new skill but attitudes are hard to change.

So how is your attitude? Do you believe in your abilities and skills or do you think you have reached the level of success you enjoy purely by luck?

Are you confident in the results you get for your clients? Do you persist in the face of overwhelming negativity?

No matter what your skillset, it is your attitude that will get you through.

**How is my attitude?**

# It Will Not Work – My TEDx Story

I was fortunate enough to be the Master of Ceremonies for TEDxMelbourne.

It was a great day. The theme was City2.0 – with unprecedented urbanisation, how do we prepare for the cities of the future.

Unlike the usual TEDx event, we were streaming some of the feed from the New York event for 90 minutes. Now, the technology was all sorted, but with a big demand for the feed we knew that there may have been issues.

So we planned for it not to work. We also planned for our backup plan not to work. The event was too important to leave to chance so we had to assume that IT WOULD NOT WORK.

When the time came, the stream was fantastic and then after about an hour it started to have buffering issues from the USA.

As MC I was up and down as it worked, didn't work, worked, didn't … Finally we killed the stream and went with our backup plan (which ended up getting a better response).

What about with what you do? Do you have a backup plan? Maybe even a backup for your backup? Whether it is a plan for the school holidays, a presentation to your boss or even a TEDxMelbourne presentation to 500 people, you need to plan for when it WILL NOT work.

# What's Your Solution?

I was up in the lovely state of Queensland visiting clients and doing some tech support for my mum and I have to say it, Mum's boyfriend is a very handy dude.

He loves working in the garden, but the sandy soil and loads of creatures up there makes for special problems. One of the solutions is to grow the strawberries in containers.

But he didn't want the containers to sit on the grass and kill it.

Also they are very heavy to lift and move, so what did he do?

A couple of old golf buggy wheels, a jockey wheel off the caravan, a wheel-less wheelbarrow, some caster wheels and a few bits of wood and steel all were made into portable plant tables. A fantastic solution that just took a bit of thinking, looking at what resources were available and what skillsets were present, to come up with a solution.

In the workplace today it seems that we struggle with solutions. We are so used to "other people" providing the solution, managers telling us what to do or giving up because "it just can't be done".

Next time this happens to you, think of my Mum's boyfriend and ask:

- What resources have I got available?
- What skillsets are available?
- What is the outcome I am after?
- How can I combine all of this to achieve the outcome I want?

# WHAT'S IT FOR?

In my role as MC I get to meet a lot of really cool people, and not just the celebrities!

Samuel Johnson was the final speaker at the plenary session of an event I attended. He is a man on a mission and he is really focussed.

I have met many business people who get to a point where they ask, "What's it for?" Their quest was to "make it", but what does that mean?

What is life for, why are they working hard, what counts, what is merely noise and why should I get out of bed today?

There are young people who experience the same thing and I suspect it is a contributing factor to a lot of the depression that people suffer.

Sam is crystal clear on what he is doing. He is living for his sister. She has terminal breast cancer and when he asked her "What legacy can I leave for you?" (expecting her to say go bungee jumping or jump out of a plane), she said to him, "I want you to ride around Australia on a unicycle and raise over a million dollars for cancer research".

So that is what he did. He ended up breaking the Guinness World Record for distance unicycling and raised over $2 million!

Sam was crystal clear on what he was doing this for and had some key strategies to get it done. What about you? Do you know what life is for? How you live your day is how you live your life so find your "why" and get cracking!

# WHAT DO I GET?

So often when I talk with people at conferences, their focus is "What do I get?" It was a delight to spend time with some people whose focus was "What can I give?"

I had the privilege of performing MC duties for 250 women attending the Emerald Community Girls Big Night In (a Cancer Council fundraiser) and the following night performing the same duties for 150 people at the Big Brother Big Sister awards night. We heard some great stories of people who willingly gave of themselves only to feel like they get so much more in return.

The workplace is the same. You need to give to others on the team before you will get what you want. Unfortunately, too many people are focussed on the pay rise, the position or the next political move rather than how they can help their customers, their team and their business get what they need and want.

Zig Ziglar said, "The best way to get what you want is to help others get what they want".

If you shift your focus from "What do I get?" to "What can I give?", you will be amazed at how good you feel and what will get dropped in your lap.

**What can I give?**

_____
_____
_____
_____
_____

# The Driver and the Dealer

At the start of each year (both calendar and financial), people get ready for the year ahead. They are planning, reviewing and getting all of their ducks in a row.

When you start to focus on your planning, don't forget the Driver and the Dealer. They are two key players in your success.

The Driver is all emotion. It allows you to tap in to the "WHY" for the year. Why do you want to earn the money, achieve the goals, or conquer the mountain? The Driver will show you the pleasure, the benefits, the reason that you do what you do. The Driver will set the direction of where you are headed.

The Dealer is all fact. It is all about the "WHAT". What do I need to do next, what resources do I need, what is the logical sequence? The Dealer is loaded with reason and logic and it is the Dealer that will get you where you want to go.

The issue is that they are not interchangeable. Particularly when you come across your first problem on the path. The Driver doesn't help because the "why" is not as important as the "What are we going to do about it?"

As you plan, make sure you are clear on your Driver and have your Dealer well-tuned and ready to go.

# What Do I Do Now?

Many people will get back in the office after a long summer vacation, and after two, three or even four weeks off, be wondering what do you do now?

Yeah, you could spend hours trolling through the email, updating Facebook or being completely overwhelmed by the to-do list that is formulating in your head or on your notepad.

My humble suggestion? DON'T DO ANY WORK!

Too many people just get back into work as if they never left. This year becomes last year all over again.

Right now is the time to get two or three key learnings from last year and do just one or two things differently this year. We need to outgrow our old self and blossom into AWESOME!

Sound good? Well here is my Regular Results Review. A simple two-page document to give you these different ideas.

Before you start any work, grab a beverage and spend the hour or so working on this so your year is loaded with great things.

You can download it here http://bit.ly/RegularResults

**What learnings from last year can I apply?**
_____
_____
_____
_____
_____

# Is That News?

I have given up watching news bulletins and I haven't bought a newspaper for years. I know for a fact that I am not alone.

Have you seen what they call news? It's like a compilation of reality TV, who's famous for being famous, and a horror movie, all wrapped up with a cute story at the end about a tap dancing dog and a funny weather person.

I'm sorry but the world is getting stupid. People now doubt scientific fact and follow self-help "messiahs" looking for answers.

There was a film released in 2006 called Idiocracy about an "average" guy who goes forward in time 500 years and ends up being the smartest person alive. It's not the best film but it is becoming scarily prophetic.

The Danish diplomat Edmund Burke said, "The only thing necessary for the triumph of evil is for good men to do nothing". I believe the same can be said for stupidity.

If we hear a falsehood being quoted as fact, why wouldn't you say something?

If governments are taking action in our name that we know are not based on facts (shark culling, reef dredging and so on) why wouldn't we at the very least sign a petition to say, "not in my name".

I am not attacking any political party and I am not pushing any political agenda. What I am doing is saying, "ENOUGH! I want my brain stimulated and not sedated. I want a world where it is okay to be smart and think for myself".

# What are You Talking About?

I am a fan of the following quote:

"Great minds discuss ideas, average minds discuss events, small minds discuss people."

It has been attributed to several different people but it speaks to me as being true.

I feel very uncomfortable sitting around with people talking about other people. Sometimes it's gossip, sometimes it's praise, but it is mostly uncomfortable, particularly if I am the one starting it! (I never said I was perfect!)

What I do know is that discussing ideas can be inspiring. They don't have to be world-breaking ideas; it may be simple principles of business, life, maths or property.

**What am I talking about?**
_____
_____
_____
_____
_____
_____
_____
_____
_____

# Are You on Focus?

Nowadays, with emails, text messages, social media, gurus popping off the internet left, right and centre, it can be hard to stay focussed on what counts.

After coming back from three days attending and hosting the National Speakers Association of Australia conference, nearly everyone I spoke to struggled with BSOs.

Bright Shiny Objects!

What about you and what you are working towards? It doesn't matter if it is a personal or a professional goal; it is too easy to get distracted. So stay on FOCUS.

Stick some posters up of what you want to achieve. Have some accountability buddies to keep you on track. DO WHATEVER IT TAKES.

**How will I stay on focus?**
_____
_____
_____
_____
_____
_____
_____
_____
_____
_____

# There is No Escape!

I was fortunate enough to be hosting a conference at Sanctuary Cove in Queensland.

Too many people can't wait to get to places like this to escape their life. They seem to feel that their business, job or relationship (or worst case scenario, their entire life) is so bad that they need to escape it for a holiday. It takes a few days to chill out and feel the sense of escape and then halfway through they remember what they are trying to escape and start to take on the stress again.

There is NO escape!

Your life is yours to create, so if you are not enjoying it or feel you need to escape it, change it! Change jobs, sell your business, work on your relationship, do whatever you need to do to address your issue. You can't avoid your life forever or you will die trying. The quickest way around is through so face your stuff and live a life you don't want to escape from.

See you in paradise!

**What great things do I need to build into my life?**

# Tough Leaders Create Tough Times

In a recent coaching session with one of my retail clients, they were recounting how times were a little tough and had been for a while. By tough times, they meant that they had not been experiencing the continual growth they used to. So it is not "OMG – let's sack people", but more of a "Hmm ... more stagnant growth, let's keep trying different ideas".

This is where their boss, the Tough Leader came in.

Usually they are really hands off and supportive. But because there is increased pressure from the board, the Tough Leader is now pressuring the area managers. More importantly, the Tough Leader is now starting to micromanage things that used to be standard processes.

Here is the problem. It is easy to lead or manage when things are going well. A few good words, the right resources and things will go well no matter what you do. When times start to get tough, a tougher management and leadership style will do more damage than good. It is in the tough times you MUST show your team and your subordinates that you have every faith in them.

It is still okay to air concerns and check on certain situations, but as soon as you start micromanaging you are undermining your team and all of the previous good work you have done. Let the person do their job and check with them what they need to make the situation a success.

Tough Leaders have a strong tendency to make tough times even worse!

So, regardless of whether you have a formal leadership position or not, are you a Tough Leader?

# GET MORE SALES

There is a very simple formula for sales:

More connections = More sales

But this doesn't mean you have to go out and find a truckload of more connections yourself; sometimes you only need to work with your existing connections to increase your sales. Selling more to an existing client or selling them additional products or services is so much more cost-effective than trying to find a whole lot of new customers.

They already know you, they already like you, and they already trust you. It is simply a matter of finding out what their needs are and then satisfying them with a product or service. (It doesn't even have to be yours! It could be a joint venture or affiliate!)

**Where can I find more connections?**

# What Do You Expect?

How many times do you hear people say, "Well what did you expect!"

Today it is your turn to contemplate that. What do YOU expect?

Working at something with the expectation that it will go the way you want it to, that you will achieve the desires or goals you are after is so much more empowering and motivating than pointing out reasons why it won't.

For today, set your expectation that everything in your world is brilliant right now and that all that you are working on will come to fruition.

Enjoy!

**What do I expect?**

# How was the Weekend?

It has been said many times that some people who want to live forever don't know what to do on a Sunday afternoon.

If you want to Get More out of your weekend, it has to be planned. I don't mean meticulously down to the last minute!

But at least have some idea of what you want from it.

- Go to the football
- See a movie
- Catch up with friends
- Visit a gallery
- Work on the house
- Rehearse your guitar playing
- Take the motorbike for a spin
- Take yourself out for brunch

The possibilities are endless, but they won't happen if you don't plan it.

**What will I do this weekend?**
_____
_____
_____
_____
_____
_____
_____
_____

# GET MORE WITH LESS

Isn't it funny when you talk with people how some people just love to talk, and usually they love to talk about themselves?

Get More from your next conversation by saying less. It's easy, just listen!

Stephen Covey refers to this as listening with intent to understand rather than listening with intent to reply.

I call it listening with respect.

I'm sorry, what was that you were saying?

**What situations need me to listen more?**
_____
_____
_____
_____
_____
_____
_____
_____
_____
_____
_____
_____
_____
_____

# When Did You Last Celebrate?

When was the last time you celebrated your success?

Not just a "Congratulations", but a real:

WAHOY! Allriiiiiiiiigghhtt Oooooooo Yeahhh!!

Well it must be time to celebrate. And not just the really big successes, but the little ones along the way. The reason you do this is because once you make celebrating success a habit, success becomes a habit.

Now that's a fun way to Get More!

**What will I celebrate today and how?**
___
___
___
___
___
___
___
___
___
___
___
___
___
___
___

# How Positive is it?

It is easy to succumb to the everyday negativity.

The news seems to cover who died and how, what terrible events happened and how things are getting worse.

The average conversation seems to be negative gossip about people around us who we don't even know.

I know you are above average! I know you want to Get More!

How about turning off the news, not reading the paper and having a conversation with a friend or colleague about the good things that are happening, what you CAN do about issues in your life and people and situations you find inspiring.

This can't help but attract more positive things in your life!

**What positive conversation topic will I contribute today?**

_____
_____
_____
_____
_____
_____
_____
_____
_____
_____

# GET MORE PATIENCE

Have you ever noticed that there are times you really want (if not demand) something to happen and it just takes longer?

You need everyone else to rush so your thing can get done?

Can't everyone else hurry up because my thing is so important?

That's when you need to say to yourself, "Don't just do something, sit there!"

Sometimes you just have to wait it out. Why not relax as you do it? Let go of other people's "stuff" and enjoy the moment of rest in a frantic world.

You may even find that what you want will happen quicker!

**Where do I need more patience?**

# FREE TROLLEY RIDE

When was the last time you had a free trolley ride?

You know what I mean. At the supermarket or hardware store just run along for a bit with a trolley, balance on the handle and call out "weeeeeee".

Can you imagine if we felt that freedom and energy every day? But the manager of the store and the manager in our head keep telling us that "You can't do that here!"

What else can you do that your head tells you, you can't? At the very least, have a free trolley ride. Everyone else will be jealous. I can hear them now, "Look at them, I want to do that too!"

**Where and when will I take a free trolley ride?**

# Take the Boat for a Spin

What makes your soul sing?
What makes you feel like you could almost explode?
What lifts your heart with so much joy you could cry?
What makes you feel connected with yourself?

THAT'S what you need more of. Make sure that you have plans in place that will bring more of it into your life.

Once you have worked out what floats your boat, don't forget to take that boat for a spin!

**What floats my boat?**

# How to Stay Focussed

How do you keep focussed?

With all the minor details crossing your desk how do you keep working towards your goals?

With all the people in your life side-tracking you with "urgent" things, how do you keep on track with what you want?

It is not easy. One way to do it is stay in bed.

Just before you get up, spend five minutes thinking about what it will be like to achieve your goals.

How will it feel, who will be there, what will it look like, where will it be?

But then you HAVE to get up!

Hurry, hurry! Don't be late!

**How will I stay focussed?**
_____
_____
_____
_____
_____
_____
_____
_____

# WHAT IF IT'S TOO LATE?

It's too late!

I should have done it when I was younger.
It should have been sent before.
If only I had done it earlier!

Usually the only person who says this is you!

The Chinese have a saying, the best time to plant a tree is 20 years ago. The second best time is today.

It's never too late. Whatever you want, start it today. You will find the results will come quicker also!

**What will I start this week?**
_____
_____
_____
_____
_____
_____
_____
_____
_____
_____
_____
_____
_____

# Just Relax!

Ever notice how people (maybe even you) get super busy and run around trying to get things done, only to find they haven't?

Ever notice that the people telling you how busy they are, seem to achieve the least?

Why not just relax? Take a deep breath and just keep doing what you need to, one little bit at a time.

Doesn't if feel soooo much better than trying to do everything at once?

Less is more ... in so many ways!

**When will I spend five minutes relaxing?**
____
____
____
____
____
____
____
____
____
____
____
____
____
____

# What Can You Do?

Have you ever noticed that sometimes we are so busy focussing on what we can't do, that it stops us from doing what we can do?

No matter how we try and drag our attention away, we keep coming back to what we can't do.

Next time that happens, stand up, walk to another room, take a deep breath, jump up and down on the spot, take another deep breath and then think about what you can do.

Yes, I know, it's weird. Yes, you may look funny. Yes, you may even laugh. That's the point. It is so weird, funny and laughable that it breaks your focus on what you can't do.

That's it. Back to it! Stop thinking – just go and do what you can do.

**What can I do today?**

# WHO DO YOU NEED?

Sometimes you have to ask for help.

I know it's hard to let go of control, I know it is hard to admit you need something, but let's face it, who really knows everything?

I have found it soooo much less painful to learn from others' experience – let them make the mistakes and I will benefit from the experience. You know what else? Sometimes as you are asking for help, you can also help others. Being open to help, assistance or just contributions from others seems to work like a magnet to attract the people you need into your life.

What do you need help with? What kind of person could help you?

QUICK! Go and help someone else and your help will be here sooner than you think!

**Who do I need to ask for help?**

# Never Mind the Rain!

Don't you hate it when you have plans for fun things to do and then the clouds come in and the rain comes down?

It was going to be soooo good, but the rain has spoiled it!

Here is a secret. Even when it is raining, the sun is still shining above the clouds. In time the rain will stop, the clouds will go and you will have a better time because now everything has been washed clean and the smell of freshness is in the air!

It's a bit like when you have things planned to do that you enjoy and something else with a higher priority comes along. Just relax and do what's in front of you. The original item will wait and be better for it!

**What do I need to let go of?**

_____
_____
_____
_____
_____
_____
_____
_____
_____
_____
_____
_____

# BE UNREASONABLE!

What excuses are you letting stop you?

What reasons do you have for not achieving or doing?

Isn't there always a reason?

"I'm too fat / thin / short / tall / white / coloured / young / old / experienced / inexperienced / early / late / sensible / crazy / hairy / bald / male / female / bossy / meek … "

The list never ends!

Be unreasonable. Don't let a reason stop you from doing, achieving or being what you want.

Go get 'em!

**Where do I need to be unreasonable?**
_____
_____
_____
_____
_____
_____
_____
_____
_____
_____

# Going Shopping?

Have you ever been shopping and come home with a whole stack of stuff you didn't want and not much you did want?

Maybe a "special" caught your eye. Maybe it seemed like a good idea at the time to get the authentic Balinese wall tapestry, but it doesn't match anything in the house or sit well within the decorative theme. Maybe the new flavoured Tim Tams looked great and you hadn't had them before so you thought you better give them a try.

Did you know a really easy way to stop these extra purchases is by using a shopping list? At a time where you are focussed on what you really need and want, you can decide what items you want to buy. Then when shopping, refer to the list to keep you on track; that way you will be sure it matches what you are after rather than just buying on impulse.

Wow! If it works for shopping, do you think it would work for your business, your workplace and your personal life?

Who would have thought it? Sitting down and spending time focussed on what you REALLY want helps you get it quicker than going at it by impulse.

So, when are you creating your strategic plan?

**What is on my strategic plan?**
_____
_____
_____
_____

# Good to be Exhausted

Isn't it great to be exhausted from doing a good job?

Whether you have spent the day in the garden digging, mowing or weeding, spent a day at the office negotiating, meeting or phoning, or spent time with family and friends talking, playing or listening.

It is actually very energising. Far more energising than just sitting there doing nothing. Watching the day go by thinking, "I really should do something". How energised do you feel when you achieve something?

Sometimes, it is what we DON'T do that drains us more than what we DO do.

Enjoy all that you do DO that you do so well!

**Where do I need to take action?**

# If You are Going, Go Hard!

Have you ever been asked to do something that you felt a little half-hearted about?

Have you chosen to do it without being sure just why?

Have you lost enthusiasm part way through?

DON'T!!

If you are going to do something, regardless of how small or inconsequential you think it may be, give it your all. You never know what may happen.

For example, my modelling agency (yes, I have a modelling agency and that is a completely different story!) asked would I work at a Pregnancy, Babies and Children's Expo. I wasn't sure. My job was to get guys to try on an "empathy belly" to see what it would be like to be pregnant. I wasn't doing anything else for those three days so I thought I would give it a go. While I was there, I thought, I will give it my best and have a lot of fun.

I had so much fun that crowds formed, the media came, the organisers loved me and then the ABC Radio (in Queensland!) wanted to interview me.

This show went on to be a major client for three years.

As they say in the classics, go hard or go home!

**Where do I need to do a little bit more?**
_____
_____
_____

# Tell Me What You Want!

As the poets of the current generation (The Spice Girls) have said:

> I'll tell you what I want, what I really, really want,
> So tell me what you want, what you really, really want,
> I'll tell you what I want, what I really, really want,
> So tell me what you want, what you really, really want,
> I wanna, I wanna, I wanna, I wanna, I wanna …

Are you that clear? Do you know what you want? What you really, really want?

Take the time to get clear. A clear focus gives inspiration and energy to achieve or attain it.

Meanwhile, I'll go listen to more Spice Girls!

**What do I want? Do I really, really want?**
_____
_____
_____
_____
_____
_____
_____
_____
_____
_____
_____
_____

# The Universe Provides

We spiritual people love to rely on "the universe" to provide for us.

Have you ever noticed though that the universe provides much quicker when you do your bit?

It is said that God helps those that help themselves (but God help those that get caught helping themselves!)

When you don't just sit and wait, but actually generate ideas, take actions, ask for help, the universe provides far faster!

Action is the magic word, not words are the magic action.

Even the universe takes action in order to provide!

**What action will I take TODAY?**
_____
_____
_____
_____
_____
_____
_____
_____
_____
_____
_____
_____

# The Most Powerful Word

There is one word that has more power, more impact and more influence than any other word. It has power regardless of language, ethnicity, belief or way of life.

That word is a person's name.

It gets their attention because they are programmed to listen for it; it influences them because as you use it you are building rapport and trust with it, yet many people don't pay attention enough to find out what it is and then remember it.

At the very least, read the person's name tag, make an effort to remember their name using some kind of association, but use it with respect, as you would have them use yours.

**Where do I need to use people's names more?**

# What's the First Thing?

A new Twitter person asked, "What is the first thing I need to do to Get More out of life?"

The answer is the same if you want to Get More Sales, Get More Growth, Get More Friends, Get More Clients, Get More Prospects or Get More Enjoyment.

You gotta have fun!

That doesn't mean you don't have to work hard, but you can have fun as you do it. Having fun makes the task easier; it makes you as a person more engaging or attractive as a friend or as a business contact.

What are you doing today to make what you are doing fun?

**How can I have more fun with what I do?**
_____
_____
_____
_____
_____
_____
_____
_____
_____
_____
_____
_____

# GETTING IN FOCUS

When I have a handyman job that needs to be done, I love going to the hardware store to find what I need. I usually end up with several things I don't need too!

Same thing happens at my desk. I start doing one thing and then bounce from one interesting thing to another until I find out that the REALLY important thing I meant to do is one of the only things I haven't done.

What is your focus today?

Stop reading this, give yourself the gift of 45 uninterruptable minutes and do that, only that, and nothing but that NOW!

Get going, what are you still reading this for?

**What is my top priority for today?**

# Make Your Mind Up!

Do you ever have to make a decision and you don't know what to do?

Do you think "a bit more time and I will know" but you never really know?

Can I humbly suggest that you choose the one that "feels" right? If both choices feel the same then toss a coin and simply do one of them.

At the end of the day, you may never make the RIGHT decision, but you will make the best decision at the time. As long as you choose to do something. Otherwise you will be years down the track still wondering which one to do and wishing you had made the decision years ago.

**What decisions can I make right now?**

# Are You Insane?

Einstein defined insanity as doing the same thing over and over, and expecting a different result.

You probably set some goals for the year. Maybe made some resolutions even. But are you insane?

What will you DO differently this year? The same thinking and actions that got you into a situation will not be enough to get you out of it. The same actions will only give the same results.

**What can I do differently that will bring me closer to achieving my goals and resolutions?**

# How is Your Perspective?

There are times when we get so distraught and upset with a situation. It can seem like it is a huge calamity and the world is against us. It is at these times we need perspective. It could be a fight with your boss, a misunderstanding with a loved one or simply a difference of opinion.

There is huge value in asking yourself, "How important is it?"

Frequently we get so fired up over an item or situation that is not important. Save your energy for the things that count.

The most important thing is to keep breathing. After that, try and step back to get a healthier perspective.

How important is it?

**What is important to me today?**
_____
_____
_____
_____
_____
_____
_____
_____
_____
_____
_____
_____

# A Frightening Question!

There is one question that puts fear into every child (and many adults!): "What do you want to be when you grow up?"

It is a question asked with care and concern and maybe even a little love, yet it is still terrifying.

The good thing is that there is no "right" answer.

For me, I think I will not grow up, as it is highly overrated. It is much more enjoyable being less serious, less concerned about things that may not happen and focussing on the fun things while still being responsible.

So next time someone asks me, "What do you want to be when you grow up?" I will simply say, "Older".

What will you be?

**What do I want to be when I grow up?**

# How BIG is it?

I think that it's a fair question. So, how BIG is it?

How BIG is your dream? How BIG is your aspiration? How BIG is your future? How BIG is the thing that gets you out of bed each day and keeps you moving forward?

We all need something. It has to be BIG. Not just big, but BIG. It has to be able to continue to draw us forward no matter what is going on. We could be having a shit day, a bad moment, some bad news, and it still has to drag us forward. So that no matter what, you can't help but do at least one thing each day to move towards it.

It has to be BIG. Beautiful, Inspiring and Great.

So, again I ask you, how BIG is it?

**What is my big hairy audacious goal?**

# You Have to Ask

I don't know about you, but I used to hope that people would offer me what I wanted. It was the polite thing to do. I didn't want to put anyone out, be an inconvenience or painful to anyone. Somehow they would miraculously read my mind and offer my heart's desires to me! Naturally, what I wanted never came my way.

You have to ask!

I have discovered that the more you ask for, the more you get. It is not being rude; it is being supportive of yourself and your own desires. Whether you are communicating to a salesperson, your kids, your partner, your pet or a work colleague, you have to ask.

If you want a discount, time off, a holiday, time to yourself, more money, a new car, to borrow a pushbike, another child, free tickets, you have to ask!

What are you going to ask for today?

**What do I need to ask for?**
_____
_____
_____
_____
_____
_____
_____
_____

# What Do You Believe?

There are many who walk among us who do things. They could be guiding what used to be multi-million dollar corporations, they may be raising kids, they may be caring for our sick and unwell, they may be cleaning up after the crowd. They do it because they believe. Maybe you walk with them?

They believe they were meant for what they do; they can't do any better than what they have; they can turn the company around; they won't fail when others have; they can continue on endlessly in the role they have or that they can build their own business.

Here is the secret: What they believe is unimportant. It is the fact that they believe that counts. Once you have belief, it can't help but come to pass, regardless if it is a positive or a negative belief.

So, do you believe? If so, what do you believe because it can't help but be true.

**What do I believe?**
_____
_____
_____
_____
_____
_____
_____
_____
_____
_____

# Time to Move

Today, like every other day, it is so easy to get caught up in what is going on. You go from meeting to meeting to phone calls to report writing to coffee to lunch to more meetings to email to strategy sessions to home.

You are not alone! I am like this too. Slowly but surely this sedentary lifestyle is trapping us. So it is time to move. It doesn't matter what you do. A brisk walk to the post office, running at lunchtime or cycling on the weekend – anything will do (jumping to conclusions doesn't count!). Some form of exercise will get the endorphins flowing, the ideas happening, the stress better handled and it can feel good.

Move it or lose it!

**How can I move more every day?**
_____
_____
_____
_____
_____
_____
_____
_____
_____
_____
_____
_____
_____

# It's Not Safe!

Just so you know, life is not safe. Accountants know about risk and return – the bigger the risk, the higher the expected return. Life is no different.

I ride a motorbike. It's a big risk – I minimise the risk with rider training, full leathers and safety gear, but it is still a risk. The return I get in terms of energy, adrenaline and a sense of being alive far outweighs the risk (for me!). Frequently the safer and less risky path brings far less enjoyment, while at other times it brings a stronger sense of security and wellbeing. Only you can choose what suits you best.

Don't be scared to take a risk every now and again. Even the safer path is not always safe.

Let me know if you want to come on a ride on the back of the bike with me!

**Where can I take more risks?**

# Are You Happy Yet?

Why is it we are never happy?

My parents were farmers and farmers always seemed to have something to complain about. The cows aren't milking, they are not eating, there is not enough feed, prices are too low, costs are too high, it's too hot, too cold, too wet, too dry, we have floods, droughts, wind … the list goes on.

Our work never seems quite right either. They are too bossy, too spineless, too confused, we need more customers, less workload, friendly teams, more focus.

I am here to tell you that there will ALWAYS be something to complain about. The secret is not to complain about it. Everything (and I mean EVERYTHING) has something good about it, even if it is simply learning what NOT to do! Shift your focus and look for the good things.

It will make life more fun and you will be much happier!

**What am I happy about today?**
___
___
___
___
___
___
___
___

# My Get Up and Go Has Got Up and Gone!

It's Monday morning. The alarm goes off and you look at the clock and think, "Just five more minutes".

That there was the problem. You took time to think.

Whenever you are feeling less than motivated it is because you took time to think about it. We can always come up with a reason why it would be better to sit and relax rather than do what we need. It is ACTION that builds motivation. Nothing motivates more than achievement. To achieve you have to take action.

Next time, don't think – just act. Get out of bed, start that report, build that pergola, mow those lawns … otherwise, you will be standing at the other side of a long list of reasons and you still won't have achieved anything.

**Where do I think too much?**
_____
_____
_____
_____
_____
_____
_____
_____
_____
_____

# LET'S GET BUSY!

How busy are you?

Many people are soooo busy and flat out that they have to spend twenty minutes letting you know about it. Meanwhile, the truly busy people are the ones who are getting things done.

So are you busy, or are you busy telling people you are busy?

**How can I be more effective?**

# Acceptance Makes it Easier

Do you have people in your life that annoy you?

Maybe they are family members, work colleagues, partners, ex-partners, your boss, friends, celebrities … the list could be endless.

My experience is that they annoy me because I want them to do things differently or say different things or just BE different. It ends up that the one who gets most annoyed is me. Bugger!

The secret is acceptance. Once I stop trying to change other people and accept them completely as they are, they then have the space to change if they want to. Most importantly I feel better and have more energy because I am not trying to manipulate and change someone who doesn't want it.

Who in your life can you "accept" just as they are?

PS: It may just be you accepting yourself.

**Who do I need to accept?**
_____
_____
_____
_____
_____
_____
_____

# How Much Extra is That?

Sometimes the best lessons in life come from the strangest places. I was reminded recently that "There is no charge for awesomeness" – yes, I know it is from Kung Fu Panda, but it is still true.

Are you "awesome"? What would it take for your customers, clients, friends, family or strangers to think that you are "awesome"? What little, unexpected things would it take?

In fact, the full quote is "There is no charge for awesomeness, or attractiveness". My experience is that the more awesome you are, the more attractive you become.

Just remember, you can't charge for it!

**How can I be more awesome for those in my life?**

# What is Most Important?

In business and in life there are many values, issues, principles, concepts and ideas that are important when dealing with others. But there is one that is the basis for success in all others.

That is trust.

Without trust:

- Your customers won't buy from you
- Your prospects won't be interested
- Your team will be less productive and wary of you
- Your boss will micromanage and check up on you
- Your suppliers will choose not to sell to you
- Your partner will hold back from you
- Your kids will not believe you
- Your friends will not support you

What are you doing to promote trust to those around you? Telling them you trust them is not enough. Your actions have to show it.

Trust me; I know what I am talking about!

**How will I show people I trust them?**

_____
_____
_____
_____
_____
_____

# How Smart are You?

It seems like an easy enough question. How smart are you?

Are you so smart that you know everything and don't listen to others?

Are you even smarter and know that you don't know everything and may listen a little?

Are you smarter than that and know that there are things that you don't know you don't know?

Some of the smartest people surround themselves with people who know far more than them. They willingly listen to new ideas, old ideas, obvious ideas, stupid ideas and any idea just to continue building their knowledge.

So I will ask you again, how smart are you?

**Where do I need to be smarter?**

# Let's Have a Meeting!

I love this definition of a meeting – "A new alternative to work".

I think it's funny but it is not true. Meetings can be incredibly worthwhile, but it is the work that is done before the meeting that makes it worthwhile.

There are a few things you need to do to make your next meeting more effective.

- Have an agenda – if it is not your meeting, let them know that if you don't have an agenda you don't go!
- Invite the correct people. Don't waste people's time by having them at a meeting they don't need to be at. If you need someone for part of a meeting, have them come in for part of the meeting and then leave. Use your resources wisely.
- Have an effective chairperson. Without an effective chairperson meetings can degrade into a series of irrelevant discussions.
- Minutes must be distributed. You need minutes to record action items and key discussion points, and those minutes need to go out no later than two days after the meeting. Minutes delivered five minutes before the next occurrence of the same meeting are a waste of time!
- Do the preparation. Know what you will be required to report on or participate in within the meeting and make sure you have done the necessary reading or research so you know what you are talking about.
- Have fun. Just because it is a meeting doesn't mean you have to be serious!

So what will you do differently for your next meeting?

# How Attractive are You?

A friend of mine has recently started attracting lots of great things in his life. He has also become a lot happier with his life and what he is doing with it. This begs the question: did the happiness come before or after the great things?

There is no 100% always-right answer.

Here is what I am doing. I choose to follow what Abraham Lincoln said, which was "Most people are as happy as they make their mind up to be". So I can choose to be happy for today. Once I have chosen to be happy, I find I spend more time hanging out with other happy people. We then talk about positive things, which builds great ideas, which inspires action, which leads to great things coming into my life.

I must be honest, it's not perfect. Some days I want to tell the world to get stuffed! Then I realise I have a choice. I choose to be happy and it makes me more attractive!

What will you choose today?

**How happy am I and how happy do I choose to be?**
_____
_____
_____
_____
_____
_____
_____

# How Much Make-up is Enough?

I had coffee with a friend in a posh suburb of Melbourne recently. I looked around and saw women who had applied their make-up with a trowel! Maybe not a trowel, but it was caked on thick. It got me wondering, how much is enough?

I understand the attraction of make-up (it is even becoming trendy for men to use it a little – manscara anyone?). It is a way to make yourself look a little better, to hide some less favourable features and highlight your assets. It seems to me that some people try to create a blank canvas and then rebuild from there. The best use of make-up is to leave your real self and highlight some bits. Others will probably not realise that you are wearing any make-up, and that way your inner beauty and authentic self can shine through.

The same can be said in business. Is your marketing message or business image so fake or so much of a cover-up that people can spot it miles away and not know who you really are? Does it completely cover the real spirit of your team and your business? How can you highlight the assets and still be authentic?

Make sure your image is based on reality. Humans have an innate ability to spot a fake a mile away!

**Where am I applying "too much"?**
_____
_____
_____
_____

# Sometimes, it Takes Time!

Have you ever just wanted something RIGHT NOW?!!

No waiting, no patience just give me the answer, the solution, the plan, what I need NOW!

I recently had some minor surgery (my gallbladder wanted out and who am I to stop it!) and I wanted to be better NOW! No waiting, no sitting around bored and uncomfortable, no long stay in hospital, I wanted to be just like Wolverine where it heals before my eyes.

Alas, that is not how life works. A friend said to me, "Don't just do something, sit there!" Sometimes, it takes time. For wounds to heal, for deals to be done, for discussions to happen, for stars to align or for hearts to mend, it takes time.

What are you trying to rush?

**Where do I need to be patient?**

# What About You?

It's the start of the week again. The weekend is just a memory and now people will want you or your work or your time.

What about you? Do you get some of your time or do you have to wait until the weekend?

It is important to set aside some time for yourself during the week. This can be spent daydreaming, meditating, exercising and relaxing, whatever you want. It is your time for you. Time for you to charge your batteries and get some sustainable energy so you don't just "get through" the day but enjoy the day.

What will you do with your time?

**How will I take time out just for me?**

# Are You Ready?

I have been working with a few of my trade show clients recently and suggesting that they get rid of the chairs in their booth. Sitting in the chair shows you are not interested, you are not right where the prospect needs you to be – regardless of whether your feet hurt or not!

The same can be said for all customer service positions, networking situations and even around the office – not that you have to get rid of your chair, but you have to be ready. You need to have read the agenda, reviewed the previous minutes, be ready to take the call, have the right questions to ask – whatever the situation requires.

So what about you, are you ready?

**Where do I need to get ready?**

# Is it Unacceptable?

Have you ever seen that (fairly ordinary) TV show, Super Nanny? Her catch-cry for the small children is that their behaviour is "unacceptable". While the show was average, the catch-cry is relevant.

Of late I have been witness to organisations whose behaviour has been "unacceptable". Why is it that as an organisation, group, team or bunch of people, we will do what we would NEVER do as an individual?

Never forget who you are and what your personal values are. Act with integrity and not only will you be able to sleep better at night, but you will be more attractive to new business, new employees, new friends and new opportunities.

On a personal level, you do not have to accept unacceptable behaviour. If you find you are, recheck your boundaries and standards to be sure of who you are and what you stand for.

Don't accept the unacceptable!

**Where do I need boundaries for unacceptable behaviour?**

_____
_____
_____
_____
_____
_____
_____
_____
_____

# What Will You Celebrate?

At the end of any grand final there are a lot of celebrations by the victors and their supporters. It is the end of a huge amount of effort over the year, a lot of training, focus and sacrifice for their goal. The team that hasn't won would have put the same amount of effort, focus and sacrifice – but they are not celebrating.

Don't forget how hard it is to ALMOST reach your goals. It is easy to get into blame mode (what the coach did or didn't do), to punish mode (I am not supporting them next year) or give up mode (that's it – I no longer care about the game!). We do the same with our own goals. We may get 98% of the way there and not quite achieve them. That is no reason to blame, punish or give up! It is a reason to review what worked and what didn't. Look at what you can do to improve and also find a reason to celebrate.

I believe that if you make celebrating success a habit, success becomes a habit. Don't focus on the 2% you didn't achieve, focus on the great things you have achieved. (Some days that can be just turning up to work!)

**What will I celebrate this week?**
_____
_____
_____
_____
_____
_____
_____
_____

# How Bizarre!

You know those bizarre experiences you have where afterwards you are left thinking, "Did that really happen?" Well I had one of those. My gorgeous wife and I went to a themed café for dinner. The food was pretty average and we decided that a "theme" was not enough to get by on. At the end of the meal the waiter asked if everything was okay – to which I gave the typical Aussie response "It was fine thanks". I didn't want to go into a song and dance routine. When we went to the counter to pay, it was the owner of the café at the register. When she asked how things were, I told her because I thought she would want to know. In particular I said my meal was ordered spicy but it was not spicy.

This is where things went bizarre. She got very angry and went on about how she told her staff to check on the client within two minutes to be sure the meals were okay. She then called the waiter over and in front of us, told him off! I was thinking, "I just want to pay and get out of here", and my gorgeous wife just hid behind me. The owner sent the waiter away, kept raving, got the person next to her behind the counter to agree with her and then we paid.

I am not sure what she was after. What she got was two customers who won't ever be going back and one upset staff member (who I hope is looking for another job because that woman is a poor boss!). She could have handled it so much better: listened to our concerns, assured us she would work with her team to make sure it's better next time, then continued training her team on what processes she wants to enable good service.

The maxim "Praise in public and reprimand in private" is as valid now as ever before. This enables the person you are talking with to maintain their dignity as well as feeling a level of respect in that you care enough to give them feedback.

How will you give your next staff or team feedback?

**Who will I give feedback to in my team?**

# 12 Days of Christmas

Welcome to the twelve days of Christmas. Maybe it's not Christmas as you read this or maybe you don't celebrate Christmas, maybe you are more a Haj, Chanukah or Bodi day kind of person. It doesn't matter; this applies to everyone.

Inspired by the "12 Days of Christmas" carol, my gorgeous wife and I came up with some ideas that spread the spirit of the season. So, rather than thinking about what your true love can give to you, my challenge for you is to think about what you can give not only to your true love, but others in your life as well.

Here is your challenge for the next twelve days, regardless as to whether it is Christmas or not. Don't forget, that they are cumulative, just like the song. That is, on the first day you give the first thing. On the second day you give the second thing and then the first thing. On the third day you give the third thing, the second thing and then the first and so on.

## **Your 12 days and their challenges:**

1. On the first day of Christmas I gave to my partner or best friend an extra long and extra firm hug.
2. On the second day of Christmas I gave to a person on the road two moments to cut in ahead of me.
3. On the third day of Christmas I gave to the person on the street $3 for a coffee treat.
4. On the fourth day of Christmas I gave to a member of my team four minutes to tell me what they thought of me.
5. On the fifth day of Christmas I gave to myself five minutes of meditation.
6. On the sixth day of Christmas I gave to my family six minutes of singing silly songs.
7. On the seventh day of Christmas I gave to my kids seven minutes of undivided attention.
8. On the eighth day of Christmas I searched my memory for eight things I learned from this year.
9. On the ninth day of Christmas I wrote in my diary nine goals for the coming year.
10. On the tenth day of Christmas I gave to my friends ten minutes of non-stop praise.
11. On the eleventh day of Christmas for my sanity I gave myself an 11-minute bath (frankincense and myrrh is optional).
12. On the twelfth day of Christmas I committed to the community 12 hours of my time as a volunteer.

It is ALMOST singable to the original tune! Don't be discouraged if you don't get it perfect, but do act on as many as you can. Carry the spirit of Christmas and giving with you as you do. I'd love to hear how you went!

# A Risk or a Gamble?

I am not a gambler. But I do take risks.

For me the difference is simple. When gambling on something, be it a business decision, personal decision or simply playing cards, I expect to lose everything. So the $20 I may spend on the card table is $20 worth of entertainment.

A risk is when I have considered the situation and taken action to minimise any negative outcomes and maximise the positive outcomes. For example, when investing I get advice from people I respect and trust, and in business, I have a full range of insurance to minimise risk.

While I am not a big believer in taking a gamble, I am a huge believer in taking a risk. The majority of the herd will play it safe and not take a risk. They will talk about it, wish they had done it, and moan about things they "should" have done, but still not take a risk.

Minimise your possibility of a negative outcome and take a risk. Doing something will have a far better return than doing nothing.

**How can I minimise my risk?**
_____
_____
_____
_____
_____
_____
_____

# Who Brought Your Success?

I want to let you know how successful my vocal group's CD launch was.

We packed the venue and had over 200 people there.
We got rapturous applause showing they liked our stuff.
Most people wanted to take us home so we sold over 100 CDs.

It was a great event and a huge success!

Now, I am not telling you this to make you jealous that you missed out (although that may happen!); I am telling you this to let you know that a huge success like this does not happen by itself. So many people contributed. Naturally, the musical director, choreographer, graphic designer and marketing manager had a significant input, but that is no more important than the individuals singing the right notes at the right time with the right words. We couldn't have done it without the venue staff looking after our guests while we sang and the cleaning staff cleaning up after we left.

Also, if our loved ones didn't support us and understand that we had to go to rehearsals every Wednesday and practise singing around the house (which is not always pleasant!), the performance would not have been as good.

So many people contributed to making us and our event a success.

What about your success? Even if you have done it all on your own, who has given you the space to make it happen? Who has put you on that path? Who has made sure you have the resources to do or achieve what you need to? Who keeps the tea and coffee stocked, the dishes cleaned, the motivation fired up, the ideas generating, the projects on track, the clothes clean, the technology running, the employees happy? The list goes on.

Once you know who they are, why not thank them? It is the little things that all go together to enable the big things to happen. Make sure you acknowledge the people who make the little things happen – because they make the big things happen.

**Who do I need to thank for my success?**

# What Do You See?

I was fortunate enough to be hosting an association conference at the Alice Springs Convention Centre.

To me, it is simply stunning. It was an awe-inspiring location.

During my conversation with other attendees, I realised that not everyone shared that perspective.

- Some only spent time inside the convention centre networking with other attendees.
- Some felt the night activities outside were too cold.
- Some thought the town centre was empty with many shops for lease.
- Some spent their afternoon on tours on both sides of the MacDonnell Ranges.
- Some felt that the weather was too good to spend inside.
- Some felt that their travel agent needed a good kick because they bought them tickets to Uluru and NOT Alice Springs (a five hour drive away!).
- Some felt the countryside was so stunning that they spent the two days driving from Adelaide to get there rather than fly.
- Some liked the place but couldn't wait to get back home.
- I am sure you have your own opinions as well.

That is the point. All too often we see something and think that everyone else will see what we see. That is NOT true. Everyone has different filters, different histories, different ideals, different values and this all impacts how they will see things.

So what do YOU see?

# It's Good

Have you seen the news lately?

Death, destruction, mayhem, questionable politicians, self-obsessed business people, profit-driven leaders, war, environmental tragedies … the list goes on and on.

Why is this in the news?

Yes, it is happening, but all the tragedy is in the news because tragedy is what rates and what makes money. Your life goes in the direction of what you pay attention to.

Can I humbly suggest that you stop watching the news and stop reading the paper? Choose to focus on some of the fabulous goodness that is going on in the world.

I have had the fortune of hosting some great events of late. One of them as Elvis (in the post-burger stages!)

The focus of these events was to celebrate the good and generate money for charity.

The people at these events are just normal people like you and me. Not super wealthy, mega-rich people, just people who work hard, love what they do and like to contribute.

At one event almost $15,000 was raised for Camp Quality and at another a cheque of $63,000 was presented to further research into spinal muscular atrophy.

It's good. Life is good.

People by their very nature are inherently good. Focus on the good, be part of the good and your life can't help but be good.

# SO WHAT IS IT?

Without knowing it, the question "What is success?" drives you. It is the reason that you do or don't do things.

Unfortunately most people have not decided for themselves what success is.

One of my long-time favourite definitions is from Ralph Waldo Emerson.

> To laugh much; to win respect of intelligent persons and the affections of children; to earn the approbation of honest critics and endure the betrayal of false friends; to appreciate beauty; to find the best in others; to give one's self; to leave the world a little better, whether by a healthy child, a garden patch, or a redeemed social condition; to have played and laughed with enthusiasm, and sung with exultation; to know even one life has breathed easier because you have lived – this is to have succeeded.

But it is still not MY definition.

I have a new exciting project coming up called Get More Success. The first step is to define what success is.

Is it:

- To earn a certain level of income
- To have regular travel
- To have a family
- To remain single
- To spend more time with certain people
- To have certain assets
- To live in a certain location
- To contribute to others
- To do all of these

Can I ask you to do me a favour? Can you please spend 15 minutes over your favourite beverage and define for yourself "What is success?"

Once you know it will be a guiding beacon for all of your actions.

**I define success as:**

# Who is it About?

Too often people in business get this question wrong, particularly in the exhibiting industry.

The answer is, it is NOT about you – it is ALL about them.

Let's be incredibly honest, no one really cares about what you do. What they care about is what you can do for THEM. That great saying of "What's in it for me" is running through their subconscious as they talk with you.

So with what you do, who is it about?

Your signs and posters, are they about you or are they about them?

Your new processes, are they about making it easier for you or making it easier for them?

Are the images you use about you or is it about them?

Your exhibiting booth, is it all about you or about them?

When you network, do you talk about you or do you talk about them?

When you get home from work, do you go on about your day or do you ask about theirs?

Life is not about you. It is about them.

The funny thing is, if you make it about them, they will happily make it about you – so everyone gets what they need.

# Where is Your Tribe?

I spent two hours this morning chatting with a friend from my tribe. My tribe is National Speakers, the association of experts who speak. It was only supposed to be an hour but once I got started, I found it hard to stop!

They understand my business like no one else does. They understand the ups, the downs, the problems, the opportunities and the excitement of running this kind of business.

They GET me.

While others will sort of get me (even my gorgeous wife doesn't fully understand the business), no one fully understands like other members of your tribe.

What about you?

Where is your tribe?

Who fully understands what you are going through?

Sometimes it is a professional association; it can also be a mastermind group or even a networking group of similar people. Whoever they are, find them, be part of them and give to them. By giving to them you will receive something no one else can give.

A sense of understanding and a sense of belonging.

So where's your tribe?

# WILL YOU SURVIVE?

Charles Darwin is often misquoted as saying "survival of the fittest".

What he actually said was:

"It is not the strongest or the most intelligent who will survive but those who can best manage change."

From what I have seen, we are not that good at change.

Look at what happens if Apple does an update or Facebook changes its interface or if the email system you use changes. People go out of their mind and spend so much energy fighting something they cannot change.

You don't have to be smart and you don't have to be strong, you have to be adaptable. It is the same in relationships and with your work.

Stop resisting change and start adapting to it. It will magnify your success and your survival.

So will you survive?

**How do I need to adapt to change?**
_____
_____
_____
_____
_____
_____
_____

# Don't be Subtle

I am not a fan of subtle – anyone who has met me could probably tell you that.

When I first got together with my gorgeous wife we created the ground rule that when communicating we wouldn't hint, suggest, imply, insinuate, infer or be subtle in any way and NEVER go down the path of "If you really loved me you would …"

The understanding is that if you want something, ask for it. If you want to do something, tell the other one, put it in the diary or organise it and tell the other one to come along. This works really well for us.

The same rules apply in dealing with your customer – internal and external.

Let them know what you need from them. Let them know what they can expect from you. Be crystal clear about it. The best relationships are when you are completely open with them and NEVER assume you know what they are thinking.

Subtle does not work. Go for clarity every time.

---

**Where do I need to express myself with more clarity?**

_____
_____
_____
_____
_____

# Again, Again, Again

Are you scared to get things wrong?

In the past, I have been so scared to get things wrong or make the wrong decision, that I have done nothing just so I wouldn't be wrong.

As part of my continual professional development, I am doing some improv training. The first thing they teach you is to celebrate your mistakes. There is no "wrong" and part of what slows you down is looking for the "right" thing. Our standard approach is that if you get stuck, stuff something up or just don't know what to do, you wave your hands in the air and shout, "again, again, again".

How great would that be in real life? Imagine if during a negotiation, part way through a deep and meaningful conversation with a loved one or simply talking with a client, whenever what you said came out wrong or you weren't sure how the next bit should go or they reacted unexpectedly to what you were saying you could just say, "again, again, again".

Next time you are scared to get things wrong, always remember you can say to yourself "again, again, again".

**When do I need to say "again, again, again"?**

# Is Your Email Worth $10,000?

One of the issues in dealing with our clients is that they forget about us.

It seems crazy, doesn't it? We deal with them regularly and then they forget about us. Sometimes it is not us they forget about, but they forget about what we can do for them and their clients.

I sent an email out to ten different bureaus, booking agencies and associations that have used me before. I wanted to give them an update on some of the things I had done in the last three months and what I had planned for the next three months.

In all honesty, it wasn't the prettiest email. It was well considered, but I didn't spend hours on it, crafting a message to inspire action and get the phone ringing. It was more along the lines of "Look at the cool stuff I have been doing and some of the stuff I am about to do. I would love to do something like this for you and your clients. If you are interested call me."

Within five minutes of sending the email, one of the recipients called me and booked a gig with me. They had forgotten that I do characters as well as straight MC work and by combining the two roles they could hit a client's budget. I also knew that if I did this well, I would keep this new client for three or four years and they do four to seven events a year. That would be worth well over $10,000 to my business.

Not a bad effort for one email.

So what do you do to remind your customers of who you are and all the things you do? It could be worth a fortune!

# The Most Productive Word in the World

A client asked me:

"How do you say no? When you're too busy, you're weighed down, your priorities rule you, but you just want to say yes to everyone. Don't want to let anyone down. You bend your life to fit them in and then you lose sleep because it just doesn't all fit.

How do you say no?"

No is the most productive word in the world.

Danielle Storey, the Million Dollar Relationships expert insists that "no opens the door to yes" and that has been my experience also.

So why don't we say it more?

There is a common saying that if you want to get something done, give it to a busy person. This is built on the concept that they won't say NO.

There are a couple of elements to this that we need to examine:

1. **Our image**

    We don't want to be seen as someone who lets another down. We want to say yes because if we don't we think that someone else will think poorly of us. That someone else could be a friend, a family member, a boss, a colleague, a new friend, an old friend or even a random stranger.

    The first thing you MUST take on board is this. What other people think of you is none of your business.

    They may think poorly of you, but if they are someone who truly values you, they will accept whatever your response is because they will know you have a lot more going on in your life than what they know about. Do you really want to spend time with someone who gets upset because you won't do them a favour? You are worth more than that.

2. **Who is asking**

    My experience is that the difficulty to say no depends on who is asking. It can be very difficult to say no to a family member. They also have the advantage of more power when it comes to emotional manipulation purely because of their history with you.

    The same can be said for a boss or a client. For some reason we think our job or the contract is at risk. As I will explain later, they both actually WANT you to say no. They just don't realise it.

3. **Self belief**

    It is so important to realise that you are worth saying no for. Too often we can see how others should say no more often, but can't see that we are in the same boat. Trust me, you are truly worth it. Your time is more important to you than it is to anyone else. Your own plans need your attention. Your own desires and needs are also important. Do not sacrifice yourself and your own needs and wants unnecessarily for others. Being a martyr is not as good as people want you to believe it is!

    I love what the flight attendants say every time I am on a plane: "When the mask falls from the ceiling, please be sure to fit your own before you assist others".

    If you don't look after your own needs, no one else will. You have to be okay first before you can be of service to others.

4. **They want you to say no**

    Without realising it, other people want you to say no.

    Most people operate on the basis that you are a mature person and when you have reached capacity you will say so. To keep saying yes when it is costing you in terms of time, energy and even sanity is not fair to you or to the business or family unit. So even though they may seem like they don't want to hear you say no, they will be much happier you did than if you come to them at the deadline and say, "Sorry I didn't get it done".

To get a bit hippy for a moment, saying no is one of the biggest acts of self-love that you can do.

By all means, please do things for other people. Please give of yourself generously, but not at the expense of yourself.

You owe it to yourself to say NO. It is the most productive and most powerful word in the world.

**Where do I need to say no?**

# What's Next?

I trust you have enjoyed the book and gained real value out of the worksheets and activities. Though the activities are not major, they lend clarity. They focus you on what needs to be done right now to gain the best results.

In all that I do, my focus is on "How can I make my client more successful?"

To this end, I have created the Get More Success program.

It is a repository of templates, tools, tips, procedures, processes, information, videos, audios and written work to address whatever situation you may come up against, as well as an active forum for members.

There is the free podcast that is issued regularly. It contains interviews with experts in their fields. You can learn something about their field as well as how they have achieved their own success.

For further information on the Get More Success program, please visit **GetMoreSuccess.com**

To find out more about how I can help you and your business Get More Success at your next conference, trade show or event please visit **WarwickMerry.com/services**

To get my weekly burst of inspiration in a style of those contained in this book please visit **WarwickMerry.com/goer**

Now it is up to you. Take action and go **Get More Success!**


**Warwick Merry**